The World of Fallout

Examining the four main single player games in the franchise and its related spinoff games, this book explores the world of the popular role-playing video game, *Fallout*.

Kenton Taylor Howard examines the maps of the games, the design of their worlds, and how the franchise has been expanded through fan-created video game modifications and tabletop games. This book highlights the importance of worldbuilding in the *Fallout* franchise, examining the extensive alternate history the game creates – diverging from real-world history in the early 1900s and resulting in a world that is destroyed by nuclear apocalypse in 2077 – and exploring how the series builds this detailed world over the course of many games. This book also examines how the franchise has served as an extended commentary on American militarism and expansionism. The series is closely examined through the lens of critical media studies, as well as relying on theoretical frameworks relating to video game design and world design.

This book will be of interest to students, scholars, and enthusiasts of video game studies, video game design, media fandom and fan studies, transmedia studies, and imaginary worlds.

Kenton Taylor Howard is a Lecturer in the Games and Interactive Media program at the University of Central Florida, USA. His research interests include video games, critical theory, and teaching. His work has been published in journals such as *Transactions of the Digital Games Research Association*, the *Well Played* journal, and *One Shot: A Journal of Critical Play and Games*.

Imaginary Worlds

Each volume in the Imaginary Worlds book series addresses a specific imaginary world, examining it in the light of a variety of approaches, including transmedial studies, world design, narrative, genre, form, content, authorship and reception, and its context within the imaginary world tradition. Each volume covers a historically significant imaginary world (in all its manifestations), and collectively the books in this series will produce an intimate examination of the imaginary world tradition, through the concrete details of the famous and influential worlds that have set the course and changed the direction of subcreation as an activity.

The World of Mister Rogers' Neighborhood
Mark J.P. Wolf

The World of The Walking Dead
Matthew Freeman

The World of DC Comics
Andrew J. Friedenthal

The World of Marvel Comics
Andrew J. Friedenthal

The World of Fallout
Kenton Taylor Howard

For more information about this series, please visit: https://www.routledge.com/Imaginary-Worlds/book-series/IW

The World of Fallout

Kenton Taylor Howard

Routledge
Taylor & Francis Group

NEW YORK AND LONDON

Designed cover image: lassedesignen/Shutterstock

First published 2024
by Routledge
605 Third Avenue, New York, NY 10158

and by Routledge
4 Park Square, Milton Park, Abingdon, Oxon, OX14 4RN

Routledge is an imprint of the Taylor & Francis Group, an informa business

© 2024 Kenton Taylor Howard

Library of Congress Cataloging-in-Publication Data
Names: Howard, Kenton Taylor, 1982– author.
Title: The world of Fallout / Kenton Taylor Howard.
Description: New York, NY : Routledge, 2024. | Includes bibliographical references and index.
Identifiers: LCCN 2023021372 (print) | LCCN 2023021373 (ebook) | ISBN 9781032498102 (hardback) | ISBN 9781032498430 (paperback) | ISBN 9781003395744 (ebook)
Subjects: LCSH: Fallout (Video game) | Computer adventure games.
Classification: LCC GV1469.25.F32 H68 2024 (print) | LCC GV1469.25.F32 (ebook) | DDC 794.8/4—dc23/eng/20230522
LC record available at https://lccn.loc.gov/2023021372
LC ebook record available at https://lccn.loc.gov/2023021373

ISBN: 9781032498102 (hbk)
ISBN: 9781032498430 (pbk)
ISBN: 9781003395744 (ebk)

DOI: 10.4324/9781003395744

Typeset in Times New Roman
by codeMantra

Contents

Introduction

War Never Changes,
But Fallout Does

As I write this introduction in late 2022, the world of Fallout is just over 25 years old – the first game in the franchise, *Fallout* (hereafter referred to as *Fallout 1*), was released in October 1997. The game's introductory video, voiced by actor Ron Perlman over a series of black and white images depicting historical conflicts, provided a quote that became the franchise's tagline: "War Never Changes." While that tagline has not changed, the world of Fallout certainly has: it began as a relatively popular turn-based role-playing game franchise created by Interplay in the late 90s; went through a period of unsuccessful spinoffs, cancelled games, and relative dormancy in the early to mid-2000s; and then was bought by Bethesda and turned into one of the most popular action role-playing game franchises of the 2010s. The most recent game in the franchise, *Fallout 76* (2018), received a less stellar reception than previous games, but the franchise remains popular, with an upcoming Amazon Prime television show planned for release in the near future and another single player game in early development.

As noted earlier, the world of Fallout has been managed by various creators over the years, making it challenging to provide an overarching summary of the games since each of those creators has approached the world quite differently. Some of the Fallout games are turn-based role-playing games, others are tactical combat oriented, with action role-playing games, crafting- and base-building games, mobile games, and many other styles all falling under the Fallout umbrella. Instead of an in-depth summary of the franchise, this chapter provides an introduction to the world of Fallout: I first highlight some elements of the franchise that all of the games share in this chapter, as well as some core themes of the series, and I then discuss more specifics about the games in later sections of this book. All of the Fallout games are

DOI: 10.4324/9781003395744-1

post-apocalyptic themed and contain some elements of role-playing, with the player typically taking on the role of a character surviving in a world after a nuclear war has destroyed essentially all of civilization. Games in the series are set during different points in the history of the franchise, which takes place in an alternate history that diverges from real-world history sometime after World War II, though all of the games are set after the so-called "Great War" between the United States and China that destroyed the world in a nuclear apocalypse in 2077. All of the games rely on an iconic visual presentation that is often referred to as "retro futuristic," depicting science fiction technologies like laser weapons and robots through a 1950s style aesthetic. There are many other hallmarks of the Fallout world as well, including dark humor, popular culture references, and perhaps most notably the iconic "Pip Boy" character who is likely recognizable even to people who have never played a Fallout game (Figure 0.1).

This project looks at the Fallout world described above, examining the four main single player games in the franchise, the most recent multiplayer prequel game, relevant spinoff games, mods, tabletop games, and other content. Fallout fits within the *Imaginary Worlds* book series due to the importance of world-building in the franchise, as the various creators involved with the series have built a detailed world over the course of many games and other pieces of media. The Fallout franchise is interesting from a world-building perspective in that a long

Figure 0.1 Fallout 1 Skills Menu; Pip-Boy can be seen in the bottom right.

running theme of its world is critiquing American politics and history while also serving as a world ripe for expansion by various video game developers, media creators, and even fans, many of whom engage with the same themes that the canonical Fallout media does. It is also worth noting that some of the Fallout spinoff games are considered noncanonical, a topic I discuss more in Chapter 3 of this book, such that what "counts" as part of the Fallout world is also frequently debated. Overall, in this book I examine the maps of the Fallout games, the design of the Fallout world, the in-universe history established within the series, and how the franchise has been expanded through fan creations such as player-created content, video game modifications, and tabletop games. I primarily analyze the series through the lens of critical media studies, as well as relying on theoretical frameworks relating to video game design and world design, which I will touch on a bit more later in this chapter.

The map of almost every Fallout game is important, and I therefore examine the map of almost every Fallout game in this book, as each game is set in a different part of the post-apocalyptic United States. From a world-building perspective, Wolf (2012: 156) argues that maps "are one of the most basic devices used to provide structure to an imaginary world," though in video games that structure is often made quite literal in that game maps typically represent the playable space within the game world. That being said, they also have an impact beyond simply being a venue for in-game action: when discussing *Metal Gear Solid V: The Phantom Pain* (2015), Murray (2018: 144) claims that "the contextualization of landscape becomes vital for what it *does*, in terms of understanding how setting (just as much as spectacular action) may drive meaning." Similarly, Murray (2018: 167) suggests that the "rule-based worlds of games are landscapes that model value systems and ethical considerations, *not only on the level of action within the place, but within the place itself.*" These notions suggest that a game's map might be as important as the actual events that take place in a game by providing both a context for narrative events and an organizational and contextual framework for those events. In a similar vein, I argue that each Fallout game's map is an important element of the Fallout world, as many of the game maps in the games offer a context for commentary on American expansionism, militarism, and history in a distinct way. *Fallout 1* and *Fallout 2* (1998) both take place in New California, which consists of California and parts of Nevada and Oregon; as such, portions of each game's map overlap, with some locations in *Fallout 1* appearing again in *Fallout 2*. I claim that this map structure allows the games to critique American expansionism by depicting the development of a small town in *Fallout 1*, Shady Sands, into *Fallout 2*'s New California Republic, a large settlement that aims to recreate an American-style democratic civilization and who is further portrayed in the spinoff game *Fallout: New Vegas* (2010). *Fallout 3* (2008) moves to The Capital Wasteland, which consists of the remains of Washington D.C. Considering this setting through the lens of critical media studies, I suggest that the world of *Fallout 3* portrays the dangers of American militarism and the downfall of American politics through a dark, post-apocalyptic aesthetic, as the in-game map centers around the destroyed United States Capitol. *Fallout 4* (2015) is set in The Commonwealth, with its map comprising Boston and the surrounding landscape. I argue that *Fallout 4*'s setting allows the series to comment on American political history through locations like the Salem Witch Museum and the Massachusetts Institute of Technology.

I also look at the design of the Fallout game worlds in this project. When discussing the job of a world-builder on a game production team, Chandler (2014: 24) claims that "gameplay is heavily impacted by the way the game world is mapped out," suggesting that the art design approach that a company takes toward a game world is a central component of game design. As such, one focus of my analysis is the shift from a 2D isometric world in the first few games by Interplay to a 3D first-person approach in Bethesda's later two games, a topic I look at in depth in Chapter 2. I suggest not only that this radical change in approach to designing the Fallout world alienated many longtime fans of the series who saw it as a move away from the series' tabletop role-playing game-inspired roots but also that using modern game production techniques led to an increase in the Fallout franchise's popularity and success. In addition, I look at the world design of spinoff games in Chapter 3, such as the mobile game *Fallout Shelter*, analyzing the different ways in which the Fallout world has been expanded beyond the RPG experience the franchise is known for. I also examine fan-created expansions of the Fallout world in Chapter 4, as fans have participated in world-building though tabletop games and video game modifications and even through systems built into games like *Fallout 76* that allow for the creation of player-generated content. In summary, I suggest that the world of Fallout is designed to be redesigned, not only by its own developers but also by other gaming companies, media creators, and even fans.

I consider the history of the Fallout world in this book as well, as it has an extensive alternate history that diverges from real-world history early in the 1900s and in which the world is destroyed in a nuclear apocalypse in 2077. In a manner similar to *Spec Ops: The Line* (2012), another game that criticizes American colonialism, the Fallout world presents "a blunt, pessimistic view of the fall of an expansionist empire" (Keogh, 2012: 12), though I claim that the history of the Fallout world also depicts the dangers of American imperialism, as it is the primary cause of the apocalypse seen in the games. Wolf (2012: 202) also suggests that "as a world grows and more narratives take place in it, backstory and world history grow as well, as narratives are linked together in the world." I therefore also look at the history of the world across the four main single player games in the franchise, as each advances the in-universe timeline, as well as in *Fallout: New Vegas*, a spinoff game that portrays what happens on the West Coast after the events of *Fallout 1* and *Fallout 2*. Overall, I argue that the Fallout world is haunted by the specter of the past, with various factions trying to remake the world based on approaches steeped in American history, and I analyze the history of the Fallout world using a critical media studies approach to draw out the ways in which the games function as a commentary on American politics.

Finally, I examine how the Fallout world extends into fan-created media, such as tabletop games and mods, as well as how some of the games enable players to create their own content. Games like *Fallout 4* and *Fallout 76* allow players to create their own structures and even settlements, establishing a framework for fan creation within the games themselves. Fallout mods, which are especially popular for Bethesda's games since the company provides official modding tools, are also another important element of fan creation within the franchise. I claim that modding not only allows fans to participate in the design of the Fallout games by expanding their worlds but also allows gaming companies to rely on modders to address issues in those worlds, taking advantage of community labor in potentially problematic ways. Not only tabletop versions of the Fallout games also offer a venue for fan creation as such games often require players to create their own characters and setting elements, but they also operate as a form of what Bolter and Grusin (1999: 4–5) call remediation, with an interesting twist because the video games were originally prototyped in the GURPS tabletop gaming ruleset.

Overall, the world of Fallout provides a number of interesting theoretical lessons for those building imaginary worlds, even outside of the realm of video games. A theoretical analysis of the Fallout world through two important critical frameworks therefore drives much of my commentary throughout this book. Critical video game studies inform that commentary, especially texts that look at violence, globalism, and politics in video games, as the Fallout world provides a rich text in terms of offering a variety of narrative elements that can be looked at through a critical media studies lens. Theories on video game design and world design are also important to my analysis, particularly since the Fallout franchise is a popular mainstream video game series that relies on many modern game design techniques. I offer an introduction to how I use each of those theoretical frameworks below, beginning by looking at texts relating to critical video game studies.

Critical Video Game Studies

As mentioned above, one primary theoretical framework informing this book is critical video game studies, which rose out of the critical media studies field, and turns to those kinds of approaches to analyze video games. Video games are a particularly fruitful form of media to analyze from a critical perspective due to the kinds of themes that are often found in them: violence being a central component of the medium is an obvious example, but games often engage with history, politics, and many other elements that are commonly addressed by critical media studies approaches. As outlined above, such elements are certainly present in the Fallout world, and the games take a critical stance toward such elements at times, though their status as mainstream commercial products often muddy that critique and raise some potential questions about its legitimacy. While I touch on broader concepts relating to critical media studies at times in this book, I primarily rely on literature that is focused on video games, and I outline some of the major theoretical sources that inform my examination of the Fallout world from a critical perspective below.

Keogh's *Killing Is Harmless: A Critical Reading of Spec Ops: The Line* (2012) is an important source for this book due to its analysis of the player's role in committing violent acts in video games. While the author acknowledges that "I actually don't really like *Killing Is Harmless* anymore" on the book's Itch.IO page due to changes he has made in how he approaches video games from a theoretical perspective, the text offers a very detailed look into the game, which is a shooter that deliberately critiques many of the violent and militaristic elements of shooters and implicates the player in that critique. Keogh's analysis provides a valuable framework for looking at similar elements of the Fallout franchise, especially in how the player takes a direct role in shaping the world and often uses violence to aid colonialist and expansionist groups in the game world. While I do not suggest that the Fallout franchise goes to the same lengths to critique video game violence that *Spec Ops: The Line* does, I do claim that it similarly implicates the player in a variety of ways, mostly notably by having many games end with a "slide show" that shows the results of the player's choices at the end of almost every game, depicting what happened to many of the game's factions and locations because of what the player did throughout the game.

The *Gaming Globally: Production, Play, and Place* (Huntermann and Aslinger, 2013) anthology also offers a useful lens into globalization and video games, and a few essays in that text provide some insights that apply to the Fallout world as well. Duncan's (2013: 85) essay looking at participatory culture and digital literacies is valuable in looking at participatory elements of the Fallout franchise that I discuss in Chapter 4, while Consalvo's (2013: 119) concept of "ludic hacking" offers a framework for looking at similar participatory approaches used in some fan mods for the Fallout games that I also discuss in that chapter. I also look briefly at McCrea's (2013: 203) discussion of the Australian video game development industry, as it touches on some of the challenges faced by Australian game developers like Micro Forte, a developer of one of the Fallout spinoff games, *Fallout Tactics* (2001), that I analyze in Chapter 3. These essays therefore offer some theoretical perspectives for some specific topics that I address in the latter half of this book.

On Video Games: The Visual Politics of Race, Gender, and Space (Murray, 2018), a book that argues that "games are potential sites for negotiating unresolved cultural, social or political frictions" (2), is another important source that informs my approach in this book. Such frictions are central to the Fallout world, as one of the core premises of the Fallout franchise is built on the notion that political friction between the United States and other major world powers leads to the apocalypse that destroyed the world and created the wasteland that all of the games are set in. In addition, many of stories in the Fallout games depict various factions that are attempting to impose their own political will on the world, leading to conflicts between those factions that create potential sites for the player to get involved in those conflicts. As such, Murray's analysis of the ways in which video games engage with politics and culture is important to this book, and I especially rely on the author's approach to game landscapes as ideology when examining the maps and history of the Fallout games. Since those maps in particular are inextricably tied to world design in the Fallout series, I also consider texts relating to world design and video game design in this book, and I outline some of the major sources I rely on from that field in the next section.

Theories on World Design and Video Game Design

In addition to theories on critical video game studies, a major component of my analysis in this book is through the lens of theories on world design and video game design. Texts on world design in general are useful for my approach: while the Fallout world was first conceptualized in video game form, the Fallout franchise is informed by a variety of media across many formats, a topic I discuss more in depth in Chapter 1. As such, an examination of all kinds of worlds provides valuable insights into the world of Fallout due to it drawing inspiration from many places and because that world has expanded into tabletop games, comics, and an upcoming television show on Amazon Prime. That being said, texts about video game design are important to my discussion of the design of the Fallout world as well, as video games are still the primary kind of media in which the franchise has taken shape and the Fallout world will likely continue mostly in video game form for the foreseeable future. In addition, some texts have even touched directly on the design of the Fallout world, making them particularly important to my analysis. I outline the major texts related to world design and video game design that inform my work in this book below.

Wolf's *Building Imaginary Worlds: The Theory and History of Subcreation* (2012) is a foundational text for this book series and therefore is also a cornerstone of my theoretical approach in this book. In particular, Wolf (2012: 12) outlines the notion of taking a world-based approach in which "a focus on the worlds themselves, rather than on the individual narratives occurring within them… can provide a more holistic approach to analysis, especially when the worlds in question are transnarrative and transmedia ones." While I do look at the narratives of various Fallout games in this book, the focus of my analysis is on the

Fallout world as a framework for narrative creation, especially since most of the stories of the individual games are driven by player choice and the results of those stories have a significant impact on the Fallout world. Wolf's analysis of canonicity is also crucial to my discussion of Fallout spinoff games in Chapter 3, as he provides a framework for looking at levels of canonicity within an imaginary world that is quite valuable given the varying levels of canonicity seen in the various Fallout spinoff games. I also more generally take a world-based approach to organization in this book: much of my chapter structure is built around how the worlds of the Fallout are designed, grouping games with world design similarities into chapters with relevant theoretical and thematic approaches rather than simply looking at each game chronologically.

Wolf's edited collection *Revisiting Imaginary Worlds: A Subcreation Studies Anthology* (2017) is also an important source that informs this text, as it provides a broad perspective on in world-building from a variety of scholarly approaches. In particular, this text looks at some specific kinds of video game imaginary worlds that that bear some similarities to the Fallout world: Landay's (2017: 128) essay on Minecraft, for example, provides a useful framework for looking at the crafting and base-building elements present in *Fallout 76* that I touch on in Chapter 4. In addition, Baker's (2017: 83) discussion of tabletop games offers an important theoretical lens for looking at how the Fallout franchise encourages the same kinds of do-it-yourself world-building that tabletop games do, especially since the Fallout world has roots in the GURPS tabletop role-playing game. Baker's essay is also useful because there have been numerous iterations of various Fallout tabletop games that I discuss in Chapter 4. I primarily draw on these two essays in this book, though I occasionally touch on concepts from some of the other essays in the book as well. *The Routledge Companion to Imaginary Worlds* (Wolf, 2017) similarly informs this project, though its approach is more conceptual, looking ideas related to world-building from numerous perspectives rather than specific imaginary worlds. Wolf's (2017: 67) essay on world design in the collection provides a useful framework for analyzing the origins of the Fallout world in Chapter 1, and Robertson's (2017: 107) discussion of history and timelines informs a similar discussion of Fallout's history in that chapter as well. Lessa and Araujo's (2017: 90) examination of world consistency also informs some of my analysis of canonicity in Chapter 3, as many of the Fallout spinoff games that I touch on in that chapter are inconsistent with the larger Fallout world.

Other than this book, Lafleuriel's *Fallout: A Tale of Mutation: Creation-Universe-Decryption* (2018) is the only book-length examination of the Fallout franchise. Lafleuriel's book also contains a forward by Brian Fargo, who was the head of Interplay when *Fallout 1*, *Fallout 2*, and *Fallout Tactics* were published, overseeing all of the original 2D isometric games. Lafleuriel's book provides a very in-depth analysis on the creation of the franchise that informs my discussion of the first two games in Chapter 1. It also provides some perspectives of Bethesda's Fallout games and some of the fan reactions to them that I touch on in Chapters 2 and 3. It is worth noting that Lafleuriel's background is in games journalism and that the book does not necessarily take an academic approach, however; this is to discount not the information contained within, but simply a note that it takes different perspectives than this book on some specific elements of the franchise. One notable example might be that Lafleuriel has a clear bias that is reflective of a more "purist" view of the Fallout franchise that I touch on in Chapter 3: the book's preface, for example, discusses the various "camps" of fans that prefer the earlier games over Bethesda's and notes that "some say that *Fallout 4* is the worst in the series" (Lafleuriel, 2018: 16). While I certainly have my own opinions about the quality of the various Fallout games, my goal in this book is to examine different iterations of the Fallout world from a world-building perspective. That being said, I will occasionally comment on the effectiveness of world-building in each game, especially in the concluding chapter of this book. Overall, Lafleuriel's book provides a wealth of information about the franchise and especially the design of the Fallout world in the earlier games, making it a valuable source regardless of the author not taking an academic approach to the series.

Sierra's book *Influential Video Game Designers: Todd Howard* (2020) is also an important theoretical text that informs my approach in this book. Todd Howard is a video game designer who is primarily associated with Bethesda Softworks, a video game development and publishing company best known for the open-world role-playing video game franchise, The Elder Scrolls. Bethesda purchased the rights to the Fallout franchise in the mid-2000s and are the current rights holders of the series, with Todd Howard serving as the lead designer on all of Bethesda's Fallout games. Sierra's text is therefore useful for providing a specific window into how the later Fallout world has been developed, offering insight into Todd Howard's approach to the franchise and how that approach aligns with the design philosophy of the earlier Fallout games. As an academic text, it is also valuable for providing information on the development of the series from an academic perspective: as noted earlier, while *Fallout: A Tale of Mutation* is quite detailed, it is aimed at a fan audience and therefore approaches the Fallout franchise from a different perspective than an academic text does. I primarily rely on this source for information about the Bethesda Fallout games, though it is also useful for information about Bethesda's The Elder Scrolls franchise as well since I occasionally touch on those games to look at the similarities between how Bethesda designed the worlds of those games and the worlds of their own Fallout games.

It is also worth mentioning one other important video game design text before continuing on simply because I make reference to the terminology used in the text numerous times throughout this book: "MDA: A Formal Approach to Game Design" (Hunicke, Leblanc, and Zubek, 2005). I highlight this text not only because it is one of the most heavily cited articles in the game design field but also because I make reference to the terms mechanics and aesthetics throughout this book, and in most cases I use those terms in the same sense as they are defined in this article. According to Hunicke, Leblanc, and Zubek (2005), mechanics are "the particular components of the game, at the level of data representation and algorithms:" essentially, a game's mechanics are its code and the rules and systems governing gameplay. The authors define aesthetics as "the desirable emotional responses evoked in the player, when she interacts with the game system" (Hunicke, Leblance, and Zubek, 2005): this definition encompasses things like setting and theme, but it is worth noting that the authors emphasize that aesthetics are higher level and go beyond whether a particular game is a fantasy or science fiction game, as they argue that a game's mood, tone, and feel are more important to the emotional experience of players. In general, when I refer to the mechanics of the Fallout world I will focus less on code and more on rules and systems. My discussion of the Fallout franchise's aesthetics will look at the setting and themes of the franchise, but I will touch on the world's mood, tone, and feel as well, especially as it relates to some of the media influences that inspired the Fallout world. I discuss many of those influences in Chapter 1 of this book, and to close this chapter I provide a brief summary of all of the book's subsequent chapters.

Book Outline

Chapter 1 focuses on the first two Fallout games, *Fallout 1* and *Fallout 2*, which were released by Interplay in 1997 and 1998, respectively. The creation of the Fallout world is the main theme of this chapter, and I highlight the Fallout world's origins in the GURPS tabletop gaming ruleset to suggest that the origins of Fallout's world are inextricably tied to the conventions of tabletop gaming, a concept I also develop later in Chapter 4 when I look at Fallout tabletop games. I also examine the maps of the first two games, which both take place in the New California region of the post-apocalyptic United States, arguing that the maps function as a commentary on American imperialism. Overall, in this chapter I claim that many of the design decisions made in the first two Fallout games still impact the franchise and are therefore central to the world of Fallout.

Chapter 2 examines Bethesda's revival of the Fallout series, with the company first bringing the franchise back for *Fallout 3* in 2008 and then making the most recent single player game in the series, *Fallout 4*, in 2015. I first address Bethesda's change from a 2D isometric perspective to a fully 3D world that primarily relies on a first-person perspective, suggesting not only that this change in world design was a risk in that it alienated many longtime fans of the series but that using modern game design techniques ultimately paid off in terms of success and popularity. I also look at the shift in setting from the West Coast to the East Coast, claiming that *Fallout 3* used its map centered on Washington D.C. to critique American politics, while *Fallout 4* similarly used its setting of Boston to comment on American history. The main theme of this chapter is therefore aimed at elements of the Fallout world that Bethesda changed when they revived the series, as well as those that Bethesda kept the same.

In Chapter 3, I examine Fallout spinoff games, which are quite numerous, though the lens of canonicity. In particular, I look first at *Fallout Tactics*, a spinoff game created by Micro Forte in 2001 and one that is often considered "semi-canon" by both Fallout fans and its developers. I then examine *Fallout: Brotherhood of Steel*, a spinoff game released by Interplay in 2004 that is explicitly considered non-canonical by both fans and developers, arguing that it illustrates some of the challenges of maintaining canonical consistency throughout a long running franchise. I then discuss *Fallout Shelter*, a mobile game created by Bethesda in 2015: its status within the Fallout canon is nebulous, as the game does not contain a traditional narrative and acts more like a simulation of an in-universe vault. I suggest that *Fallout Shelter* therefore functions as a metanarrative about the Fallout canon rather than a true expansion of the Fallout world, operating in a state I refer to as *metacanonicty*. Finally, I analyze *Fallout: New Vegas*, which was created in 2010 by Obsidian Entertainment and is considered the only fully canonical spinoff game: I claim that *Fallout: New Vegas* continues the critique of American imperialism established in the first two games. Overall, I not only suggest that the world of Fallout is designed to be redesigned but also claim that Fallout spinoff games are most successful when they stay true to the canon and spirit of the Fallout world.

The focus of Chapter 4 is fan creation in the Fallout franchise. I first look at *Fallout 76*, a multiplayer spinoff game created by Bethesda in 2018, suggesting that the significant negative reaction to *Fallout 76* stemmed from Bethesda reinventing core elements of the Fallout world, but that the game's reliance on player-generated narratives continued a long running theme of reinvention and expansion of the world of Fallout by people other than its creators. I then consider mods for the Fallout games, claiming that mods allow fans to expand the Fallout world in even more significant ways. I also argue that while allowing fans to expand the Fallout world through modding is a good thing, it enables gaming companies to take advantage of community labor by relying on modders to fix problematic gameplay or narrative components of the Fallout world. Finally, I address Fallout tabletop games, which are an interesting example of remediation in that they remediated a digital game into an analog setting, an example made even more interesting due to Fallout's origins in the GURPS tabletop ruleset. The main goal of this chapter is to tie together these various fan-created expansions of Fallout's world: while player-created narratives, mods, and tabletop games are all different ways for fans to engage with Fallout, they all operate as expansions of the Fallout world that go beyond the official stories told in the video games, allowing fans themselves to participate in the franchise's world-building.

Finally, in the concluding chapter, I examine the world of Fallout from a broader perspective, focusing on the successes and failures of world-building within the franchise. My goal here is not to praise particular games and criticize others but to instead explore the design lessons that can be gleaned from the world of Fallout's commentary on American politics and history. Some of these lessons are more game-focused due to the franchise itself working within that medium, but others are general enough that anyone interested in exploring other imaginary worlds can benefit from them as well. I also take a brief look at these lessons in the context of *All Roads* (2010), a *Fallout: New Vegas* prequel comic, Fallout Pinball, an expansion pack for *Bethesda Pinball* (2016), and the upcoming Fallout television show. Overall, I argue that the world of Fallout demonstrates the potential of imaginary worlds to critique the real world's politics and history.

References

Baker, Neal. 2017. 'Secondary World Infrastructures and Tabletop Fantasy Role-playing Games,' in *Revisiting Imaginary Worlds: A Subcreation Studies Anthology*, edited by Mark J.P. Wolf, pp. 83–95. London: Routledge.

Bolter, Jay David and Grusin, Richard. 1999. *Remediation: Understanding New Media*. Cambridge: The MIT Press.

Chandler, Heather Maxwell. 2014. *The Game Production Handbook*, 3rd edition. Burlington: Jones and Barlett Learning.

Consalvo, Mia. 2013. 'Unintended Travel: ROM Hackers and Fan Translations of Japanese Video Games,' in *Gaming Globally: Production, Play, and Place (Critical Media Studies)*, edited by Nina B. Huntermann and Ben Aslinger, pp. 119–139. New York: Palgrave-McMillian.

Duncan, Sean C. 2013. 'Snapshot 3: Crafting a Path into Gaming Culture,' in *Gaming Globally: Production, Play, and Place (Critical Media Studies)*, edited by Nina B. Huntermann and Ben Aslinger, pp. 85–89. New York: Palgrave-McMillian.

Hunicke, Robin, LeBlanc, Marc and Zubek, Robert. 'MDA: A Formal Approach to Game Design,' in *Proceedings of the AAAI Workshop on Challenges in Game AI*, 4(1), pp. 1722–1727.

Huntermann, Nina B. and Aslinger, Ben (eds.) 2013. *Gaming Globally: Production, Play, and Place (Critical Media Studies)*. New York: Palgrave-McMillian.

Interplay Productions. 1997. *Fallout: A Post Nuclear Role Playing Game*. Interplay Productions.

Keogh, Brenden. 2012. *Killing Is Harmless*. Marden: Stolen Projects.

Lafleuriel, Erwan. 2018. *Fallout: A Tale of Mutation: Creation – Universe – Decryption*. Toulouse: Third Editions.

Landay, Lori. 2013. 'Minecraft: Transnational Objects and Transformational Experiences in an Imaginary World,' in *Revisiting Imaginary Worlds: A Subcreation Studies Anthology*, edited by Mark J.P. Wolf, pp. 127–148. London: Routledge.

Lessa, Rodrigo and Araújo, João. 2017. 'World Consistency,' in *The Routledge Companion to Imaginary Worlds*, edited by Mark J.P. Wolf, pp. 90–97. London: Routledge.

McCrea, Christian. 2013. 'Snapshot 4: Australian Video Games: The Collapse and Reconstruction of an Industry,' in *Gaming Globally: Production, Play, and Place (Critical Media Studies)*, edited by Nina B. Huntermann and Ben Aslinger, pp. 203–206. New York: Palgrave-McMillian.

Murray, Soraya. 2018. *On Video Games: The Visual Politics of Race, Gender, and Space*. London/New York: I.B. Tauris.

Robertson, Benjamin J. 2017. 'History and Timelines,' in *The Routledge Companion to Imaginary Worlds*, edited by Mark J.P. Wolf, pp. 107–114. London: Routledge.

Sierra, Wendy. 2020. *Todd Howard: Worldbuilding in Tamriel and Beyond (Influential Game Designers)*. London: Bloomsbury Academic.

Wolf, Mark J.P. 2012. *Building Imaginary Worlds: The Theory and History of Subcreation*. London: Routledge.

Wolf, Mark J.P. (ed.) 2017. *Revisiting Imaginary Worlds: A Subcreation Studies Anthology*. London: Routledge.

Wolf, Mark J.P. (ed.) 2017. *The Routledge Companion to Imaginary Worlds*. London: Routledge.

Wolf, Mark J.P. 2017. 'World Design,' in *The Routledge Companion to Imaginary Worlds*, edited by Mark J.P. Wolf, pp. 67–73. London: Routledge.

1 Origins of the World of Fallout

Fallout 1 and *Fallout 2*

In the introduction to this book I discussed some of the key themes in the world of Fallout, looking at how those themes show up across the franchise's 25-year history. Fallout has been a remarkably consistent imaginary world, and even though many different developers have tried their hand at making Fallout games, most of those games still address the main themes of the Fallout series. Of course, the world of Fallout has evolved over time, and the most recent game in the franchise, *Fallout 76* (2018), looks quite different than the first two releases in the series, 1997s *Fallout* and the 1998 follow-up, *Fallout 2*. That being said, some of the core themes of the Fallout world are still present in more recent Fallout games, and I suggest that this is likely because the first two games establish some core elements of the franchise, such as its retro futuristic visual theming, that have become so thoroughly associated with Fallout that it would seem impossible to make a Fallout game without such elements. I look at those elements in this chapter to provide a framework for looking at similar elements in the later Fallout games in future chapters of this book.

In this chapter I discuss the origins of the world of Fallout by looking at the first two games in the series, *Fallout* and *Fallout 2*. While the first game in the franchise is simply titled *Fallout*, throughout this book I refer to the first game as *Fallout 1* for clarity's sake to distinguish between a specific discussion of the first game and a more general discussion of the Fallout franchise itself. I look at both games in this chapter together because they were released within a year of one another and were mostly created by the same development team using the same game engine; as such, many elements of the two games are very similar and form some of the foundations of the Fallout world. I first examine the origins of the franchise, looking at various media inspirations cited by the Fallout world's original creator, Tim Cain,

DOI: 10.4324/9781003395744-2

and especially at GURPS, the tabletop game ruleset that *Fallout 1* originally used as the basis of much of its game systems. I then look at the map of each game and how the games use their worlds to comment on American politics by depicting the growth of a small frontier town into an expanding democratic colonial civilization. Overall, in this chapter I argue that the series' origin in a tabletop gaming ruleset influences world-building throughout the franchise and that much of the series' ongoing criticism of American colonialism and militarism began with narratives and world design elements established in the first two games.

From GURPS to S.P.E.C.I.A.L.: The Importance of Tabletop Influences on the World of Fallout

Unlike some imaginary worlds, detailed information on the creation of the Fallout world is easy to find, as many of the game's developers have spoken openly about it. One of the best sources for such information is Tim Cain's "Classic Game Postmortem: Fallout," a talk delivered at the Game Developer's Conference (GDC) in 2012 that provides a window into the early conceptualization and design of the world of Fallout. According to Cain (2012), development on *Fallout 1* began in 1994, and the team working on the game started with one person, Cain, before growing to about 30 people or so over the course of the game's three-year development cycle; as such, much of the early world-building for the Fallout world was done by Cain himself. The project was unique in a couple of ways: Interplay games of that time usually were usually based on licensed properties, especially the Dungeons & Dragons (D&D) franchise, and were typically developed in an existing engine such as the Infinity Engine; on the other hand, *Fallout 1* was an original intellectual property and Cain (2012) claims that he developed an entirely new engine for the game. This meant that the conceptual design of Fallout's world differed greatly from other Interplay games at the time: most other games the company was making in the mid- to late 1990s were not only created using their license to make D&D video games but often took place in specific locations within established fantasy worlds that make up the franchise, most of which have a great deal of existing canon in places like various D&D books. As an example, *Baldur's Gate* (1998), a game which Interplay was working on at the same time as *Fallout 1*, is the name of a specific city within the popular Forgotten Realms campaign setting, one of D&D's

most popular worlds: the developers of *Baldur's Gate* were therefore able to rely on the vast amount of extremely detailed existing source material about the game world they were creating, and Interplay's support for the project was based on the assumption that a large built-in fanbase would ensure success for the game. The Fallout world, on the other hand, was a wholly original franchise and had to be created from scratch, and as such Cain was tasked with building a new video game series that did not have the same kind of support that other Interplay games of the time had. The conceptual phases of Fallout's world design therefore drew primarily on various kinds of media that influenced Cain and other members of the design team, and those influences can be seen at many different stages during the game's development, as well as in the finished game. I examine those influences below to argue that while they were all important *Fallout 1*'s tabletop game influences were the most impactful on world design in the franchise as a whole.

Influences from other media were important during the early design of Fallout's world: while discussing the development of the first game, Cain (2012) noted that the team making the game was very "media-spongey" and mentioned specific book, movie, and game influences that they drew from while building the world. Looking at these influences therefore offers insights into the design of Fallout, though I claim that some of these influences did not necessarily impact its world design as much as others. In his postmortem, Cain (2012) mentions three main books that inspired the Fallout franchise: Walter M. Miller Jr.'s science fiction novel *A Canticle for Leibowitz* (1959), Richard Matheson's horror novel *I am Legend* (1954), and Nevil Shute's apocalyptic novel *On The Beach* (1957). All three books primarily offered thematic inspiration for certain story beats in *Fallout 1*, as Cain highlights particular moments in the game that are drawn from each book. In terms of movies, most of the influences Cain mentions inspired the visual language of the Fallout world. Cain highlights George Miller's post-apocalyptic film *The Road Warrior* (1981) as an inspiration, with *Fallout 1* containing multiple visual references to the movie, as the game's leather jacket and dog sprites are both drawn from the film (Figure 1.1).

Similarly, Fred M. Wilcox's science fiction film *Forbidden Planet* (1956) inspires much of the visual presentation of the Fallout world's science fiction elements, such as robots and energy weapons, which resemble 1950s era depictions of such technologies. Marc Caro and Jean-Pierre Jeunet's French science fiction film *City of Lost Children*

(1995) is also mentioned as an inspiration for the appearance of *Fallout*'s iconic power armor helmet, an image that appears on the box art of almost every game in the franchise (Figure 1.2).

Figure 1.1 Player character wearing leather jacket standing next to a dog.

Figure 1.2 Fallout 2's main menu; Power Armor helmet can be seen in the bottom right.

Overall, these books and film inspirations impacted the theming and visuals of the Fallout franchise, elements that are at least somewhat related to the design of the Fallout world, though since the franchise's visual design has changed significantly over time some of those influences may be less important, especially on the later Fallout games.

Computer games more directly inspired world design in the Fallout franchise, with some of *Fallout 1*'s computer games inspirations mostly impacting the game's mechanics. Mechanics are related to world design in games since a game's rules influence the way its world is constructed: Murray (2018: 153) notes when discussing game worlds that "these generated landscapes are designed with play in mind, skewed in order to design a curated gameplay experience." A good example of this kind of influence would be Mythos Games' video game *X-COM: UFO Defense* (1994), which was a major influence on how *Fallout 1*'s combat system worked early in development: Cain (2012) claims that the game's combat was very similar to *X-COM's* until they got the license to use the GURPS tabletop gaming ruleset and converted the game's rules over to that system. This mechanical impact was retained throughout the various redesigns that *Fallout 1* went through, as *X-COM's* combat is still a clear influence on the turn-based tactical nature of combat in *Fallout 1* and the other early Fallout games, and it impacts world design because maps in the early games are constructed with tactical combat in mind. Cain also mentions Interplay's video game *Wasteland* (1988), a game which is likely the most well-known influence on the Fallout franchise, as Cain describes *Fallout 1* as a "spiritual successor" to *Wasteland,* a claim that has been echoed by many people associated with the original game. *Wasteland* therefore had more of an impact on the Fallout franchise's world design than X-COM did, and in quite a few different ways: Lafleuriel (2018: 21) argues that "*Wasteland* was the inspiration for more than just *Fallout's* post-apocalyptic setting," noting a few important other elements such as *Wasteland's* "innovative tone and features." I argue that while *X-COM* was a mechanical influence on the world of Fallout, *Wasteland's* influence was primarily aesthetic: rather than just inspiring the combat system or setting, Wasteland inspired the mood of the Fallout world. Even more importantly, *Wasteland* and Origin Systems' game *Ultima III: Exodus* (1983), another inspiration mentioned by Cain, are both heavily influenced by tabletop games, which I claim are the most significant form of media that inspires the Fallout franchise in terms of world design.

The computer game, book, and film influences Cain mentions in his GDC talk provide a useful look into some elements of world design in

Fallout, but I argue that Fallout's world design is very closely tied to the tabletop role-playing game influences that Cain discusses, even more so than the other influences. One such influence is the Gamma World franchise, a post-apocalyptic tabletop game series that is closely related to the D&D franchise: most of the various editions published over the years have been published by the same company that was publishing D&D at the time, and in most cases the game's rules have been mechanically compatible with the then-current version of D&D. Gamma World was primarily an aesthetic inspiration for the Fallout franchise, much like the video game *Wasteland* was, in that elements of Gamma World such as mutations spawned by radiation and the world being destroyed by a cataclysmic event inspired similar elements in the world of Fallout. Gamma World is less influential on the Fallout world's mechanical design; however, as much like other tabletop role-playing games, most versions of Gamma World have the player select a character class that influences the type of character that the player creates, which was something that Cain (2012) and the rest of the team specifically wanted to avoid in Fallout, describing classes as "stereotypes" for characters. That being said, Gamma World's impact on the Fallout franchise is undeniable, especially since it was an early attempt at providing an alternative to fantasy-themed role-playing games like D&D, something the Fallout team was likewise doing by breaking away from the D&D-based video games Interplay was making at the time.

The most influential tabletop gaming system on the world of Fallout is GURPS, the tabletop ruleset that was originally going to be used in the Fallout series. GURPS, or Generic Universal Roleplay System, is a tabletop gaming ruleset created by Steve Jackson Games, and as Lafleuriel (2018: 28) puts it, "Cain based all of [*Fallout 1*'s] gameplay on the GURPS RPG rules." Unlike many other tabletop gaming systems, which often have specific genre elements and theming built into the system, GURPS is designed as a system that is setting-agnostic: a GURPS game could be set in a fantasy world much like a D&D game, but it could also be set in a science fiction world, a modern world, a historical world, or in almost any other kind of setting. Because of this lack of a specific setting, GURPS was designed differently than many other tabletop games of the time: in particular, character creation in GURPS is set up to be setting agnostic as well and therefore can be used to create a wide range of character archetypes across a variety of genres. Character classes are also not used in GURPS, as in most tabletop role-playing games those character classes are setting specific: for example, the Wizard and Druid classes in D&D are based around medieval fantasy tropes. GURPS characters are instead typically defined by statistics like Strength that determine their physical and mental capabilities and skills like Pilot (Modern era aircraft) that describe tasks that the character can successfully accomplish. Lafleuriel (2018: 29) notes that "according to Fargo, the team liked this rules system because it included mechanisms that highlighted the characters' personalities." Similarly, Cain (2012) claims that GURPS was particularly influential in terms of Fallout's character creation mechanics: *Fallout 1* was originally intended to be built within the GURPS system, and the Fallout world's use of a classless-, skill-, and stat-based character creation system is drawn directly from GURPS. As such, a connection to tabletop role-playing games is inherent to the Fallout world, and while character creation is handled differently in later Fallout games, many elements from *Fallout 1*, such as the S.P.E.C.I.A.L. statistics system, are still in place.

While using a classless system for character creation may seem to be only a mechanical choice in terms of game design, such an approach also significantly impacts world design in a video game: since characters in such a system might not fall into established character archetypes as they typically will in a class-based system like D&D, the world must be designed with ample opportunities for the system's various statistics and skills to be used within the game world. Even the skills available in such a system have an impact world design: for example, Fallout features skills such as "Lockpick," "Repair," and "Traps," which requires creating a world with locked doors, damaged objects, and trapped areas. As such, the choice of a tabletop-based, open-ended character design system based on GURPS impacted the design of Fallout's world significantly during the early stages of development, and even after disagreements lead to Fallout losing the GURPS license, the game world was still designed around a classless character creation system intended to give the player a significant number of options for defining a particular character archetype. This approach has also been retained throughout all of the Fallout games, making it one of the most central elements of its world design: gameplay throughout the franchise's history has evolved dramatically, but classless-, stat-, and skill-based character creation is a core tenet of the franchise and only a few Fallout games have strayed from that approach.

While GURPS was influential on the development of the Fallout world, a particularly impactful moment also occurred when the team lost the GURPS license. During the second year of development the team got the license to use the system, as Cain was particularly passionate about making the Fallout world using GURPS-based mechanics (Cain, 2012). Steve Jackson Games, the owner of the GURPS license, disliked the art style and level of violence in *Fallout 1*, however, and the game was far too late in development to make any changes to those elements (Cain, 2012). At that point, Lafleuriel (2018: 30) claimed that "*Fallout* was now without a game system and faced the very real risk of being cancelled and dropped," and the team was given two weeks to redesign *Fallout 1*'s GURPS-based game systems into something wholly original. Facing potential cancellation, the team accomplished the task, creating the S.P.E.C.I.A.L. system that remains in use in the Fallout franchise today (Cain, 2012). GURPS was stripped out of the game at a relatively late stage in development, however, and its influence can be felt throughout the Fallout world: for example, player statistics in GURPS are derived from a character's Strength, Dexterity, Intelligence, and Health statistics, which see equivalents in Fallout's Strength, Agility, Intelligence, and Endurance statistics, with Fallout adding Perception, Charisma, and Luck statistics. Skills in GURPS are setting dependent and open ended, with the aim of offering skill that governs almost any task a player might want to do: a medieval setting might have skills like Riding and Smithing, while a modern setting might offer Piloting and Engineering skills instead. While Fallout's skills are based on its specific post-apocalyptic setting, they are similarly aimed at offering a broad variety of options: the first game offers 18 skills, with many of the subsequent games offering even more. As mentioned earlier, this wide variety of skills has an impact on Fallout's world design, as opportunities must be created to use those skills throughout the game world, but unlike other Interplay games, Fallout did not have an existing world to be based on. In fact, much of Fallout's specific aesthetics came relatively late in development, a topic I discuss further in the next section.

Building the World of Fallout: The Map and Timeline of *Fallout 1*

Before discussing the map and timeline of *Fallout 1*, it is worth noting that the choice of a post-apocalyptic setting based off the real-world western United States was a fairly late design decision. Cain notes that the team considered many potential settings early on: in fact, many members of the team wanted to use a fantasy setting in an attempt to out-do the current popular D&D-based games of the time and because many of those team members had previously worked on fantasy games (Cain, 2012). That idea was scrapped because of how many other popular fantasy RPG franchises were around at the time: as Lafleuriel (2018: 24) notes, "the team wanted to make a fantasy title, but the market was already inundated with them." A time-travel-based game was considered next, in which the player would move through various settings, including the modern era, prehistory, and the future, an idea that was mostly abandoned due to issues with the game's scope and the budget that would be necessary to create such a game (Cain, 2012). A plan for an alien invasion-oriented game came next, in which players inhabited the last remaining city on a devastated Earth: this concept seemed to push the team toward the world design used in the Fallout franchise, and Cain notes that those ideas inspired the concept of Vaults in the world of Fallout (Cain, 2012). From there, Cain (2012) notes that the team settled on a post-apocalyptic world specifically because they wanted to make a sequel to *Wasteland*, a goal that Interplay's owner at the time, Brian Fargo, also supported: in fact, they attempted to get the license for the game from Electronic Arts, the owner of the *Wasteland* license at the time, for well over a year. Their lack of success may have simply been due to the fact that *Wasteland* was an influential game: Lafleuriel (2018: 21–22) notes that the game "had a lasting impact on the market, and its reputation perhaps explains why Brian Fargo found it impossible to obtain the license from Electronic Arts to make a sequel." While they were unable to work out any kind of licensing agreement for *Wasteland*, Cain's team and Interplay liked the idea of continuing to work with a post-apocalyptic world (Cain, 2012). Fallout's setting was therefore the result of iteration, with some elements of its world design being inspired by the team's previous failed attempts at creating a wide variety of different potential worlds. This is unsurprising given that iteration is a core element of game design: for example, Fullerton (2018: 16) argues that "iteration is deeply important to the playcentric process." That being said, I suggest that iteration being at the core of the franchise's world design might explain why there have been so many various expansions of the Fallout world.

The world map of *Fallout 1* centers on Southern California, mostly in the area surrounding the city of Los Angeles, which is referred to as The Boneyard and has a small remaining human population, operating as a town that the player can visit. The player comes from Vault 13, an underground bunker that provides a safe haven for a small number of people and that has remained almost entirely separate from the post-apocalyptic outside world. Junktown and The Hub serve as major cities and the primary bastions of civilization in the area that the player can visit, with each town having functional commercial and political systems, as well as guards or police forces that offer a modicum of protection. Shady Sands, a small town near the player's starting location, is also worth mentioning here simply because it is only other settlement in the area – but I will touch more on Shady Sands later in this chapter, as the unassuming village is quite important to the world of Fallout and warrants a more thorough discussion. There are also other locations scattered across the map, most of which function much like dungeons in other video games in terms of providing challenges that the player must complete in order to achieve in-game objectives: for example, the destroyed ruins of the city of Bakersfield are now known as the Necropolis and are populated by radiated humans called ghouls as well as the notoriously dangerous Super Mutants, and the player must navigate the location in order to acquire a water chip needed to repair computer systems within Vault 13. The map is based on the part of real-world America, offering the game an opportunity to portray a post-apocalyptic version of American politics and society and use that portrayal to critique elements of real-world politics, though before looking at how the game does so it is also important to briefly consider the history of the Fallout world before the first game began for context about how that commentary develops in *Fallout 1* and throughout the rest of the games.

The timeline of the Fallout world differs from real-world history in a few key ways that are worth addressing. Wolf (2017: 67) argues that "practically all imaginary worlds begin with the template of the Primary World, the world we live in, gradually replacing its default assumptions and structures with invented material." This is the case in the Fallout franchise, which begins with the template of the Primary World but replaces some historical events with others. In particular, some important events in American history are altered in the Fallout universe: for example, November (2013: 299) points out that "in *Fallout*, the United States won the race to put a man in space, emerged victorious in Vietnam, and saw no social upheaval in the late twentieth century." Of course, the games depict the United States as having fallen into a post-apocalyptic wasteland and are set well after these historical alterations: how the apocalypse happened is not entirely clear, though there is some information about the event found in the games and in the Fallout Bible, an unofficial document put together by *Fallout 2* developer Chris Avellone that collected and expanded on various elements of the Fallout canon as a reference for people working on later Fallout games. As a high-level summary, a large-scale conflict called the "Resource Wars" lead to the world being destroyed during a nuclear exchange between the United States and China in 2077 dubbed "The Great War:" from all accounts, this exchange eliminated essentially all major societies on the planet. The American government and military worked with a corporation called Vault-Tec to build enormous underground Vaults to protect the population from such an event, but there were not nearly enough to house all of the populace, and the ones that were built were secretly constructed with the goal of performing social experiments on those living within them. Obviously, these events differ from the Primary World and much of Fallout's timeline is set in the future, though they present some themes that the Fallout world relies heavily on in its critique of American militarism and politics.

The situation laid out in Fallout's alternative timeline is an obvious critique of the American military industrial complex, but the fact that it leads to an apocalyptic event that is a core part of the Fallout world's history makes it an undercurrent that runs throughout all of the franchise. Robertson (2017: 107) argues that "timelines might simply be understood as pointing to a set of events from a world's past upon which the very possibility of narrative in that world is based," and "The Great War" creates a narrative premise built around a criticism of American militarism. This criticism has been noted before and can be seen from a variety of perspectives: for example, McClancy (2018) argues that "*Fallout* creates a simulacrum that justifies the policies of the Global War on Terror." Designer Tim Cain highlights this element of the world as well and even notes that a critique of politics was intentional, saying that

> We made it quite clear that the government was lying to you. The military and corporations like Vault-Tec had seized power. These companies profit from the fear of war, and if war really broke out, they planned on profiting again. It wouldn't hurt if the game inspired players to view their own real government with a more critical eye.

> (Barton, 2010)

In 2161, when the main character of *Fallout 1* first leaves their vault, the events of The Great War are still apparent almost 100 years later: while there are a few beacons of civilization on the first game's world map as mentioned earlier, these are few and far between, and life in those few settlements is depicted as harsh and desperate for most people. Radiated monsters roam the areas between towns, making travel dangerous, and even some of the towns themselves are under attack by raiders, criminals, or deadly creatures. While information about the wider world is scarce in the first game, the implication is that the situation is similar everywhere, an implication that turns out to be mostly true based on the canon established in later Fallout games. The Fallout world therefore presents a stark commentary on the dangers of the American military industrial complex, implying that it might lead to long-lasting devastation for all of humanity; it then continually reinforces that commentary throughout its world design.

While these general elements of the Fallout map and timeline are an obvious commentary on American militarism, a more specific example can be seen in how the world of Fallout is transformed during the events of *Fallout 1* and *Fallout 2*, which takes place 80 years after the first game. In particular, I focus here on the depiction of events surrounding a small town in *Fallout 1* that I mentioned earlier: Shady Sands. In *Fallout 1*, Shady Sands is most likely the first location that the player visits after leaving Vault 13 at the beginning of the game. The town is located just east of Vault 13, and when the game begins, the player is directed to head east and explore another nearby vault, Vault 15, for potential clues about the whereabouts of the water chip the player has been tasked with finding. Shady Sands sits directly between the two vaults along the player's path, such that it presents itself as an obvious stopping point on the journey to Vault 15. As Dunne (2018: 63) notes, "this was an intended design decision," as Dunne interviewed Tim Cain as part of his doctoral thesis, and Cain claimed that

We did that deliberately for *Fallout 1* and we did it in *Fallout 2*. We would tell you [the player] to go one place and you'd get it marked on the map and then have to go [to] another place that we'd deliberately place [en route]. So you were going along and the map would

> automatically stop and go, 'You see a town.' And you're like, 'Oh,
> I'm going to go there.'
>
> (Dunne, 2017: 177)

Assuming the player stops at Shady Sands, they will find a small
frontier town eking out a difficult existence in the wasteland and beset
by various problems, a story thematically matching that of many early
American colonial narratives and a common situation encountered
in role-playing games. The player can solve those problems, one of
which being a group of raiders who regularly threaten the populace.
Both Shady Sands itself and those raiders, who live in a nearby base
and call themselves the Khans, are the remnants of the original inhabitants of Vault 15 who left and formed various communities in the
wasteland. It is also worth noting that Vault 15, like many other vaults,
was designed as a social experiment: it was deliberately populated
with people of radically differing backgrounds and ideologies to see
what would happen if such a group of people was forced to live in a
cramped, isolated underground space. This unsurprisingly did not go
well, with the inhabitants dividing into different factions: some of the
inhabitants left and took much of the vault's technology with them,
while others left to form raiding groups. The implication is that Shady
Sands represents the group that used the technology that brought with
them to create a town, while the Khans represents another group that
survived by raiding the nearby area.

The resolution of the Shady Sands and Khans storyline is an important one, mostly because while the results of the conflict in *Fallout 1*
are obviously dependent on the player's actions, both groups appear
again in *Fallout 2*, the storyline of which suggests some specifics about
how events turned out in the first game, presenting a canonical version of the Shady Sands–Khans storyline even though that storyline
is dependent on player choice. It is also worth noting that I previously
discussed this issue in a nonlinear web-based essay built in Twine, an
interactive fiction scripting program, noting the challenges of analyzing a game with different potential outcomes in a linear format and
arguing for a nonlinear approach to such games (Howard, 2019). That
being said, I do not take such a nonlinear approach here: while I will
discuss potential alternatives to the canonical outcome of this story
below and will discuss the implications of this storyline on *Fallout 2*
in more detail in the next section, I will approach the overall canon
of the Fallout world with the assumption that these events play out in

the same way as they are told to the player in *Fallout 2*, as they are a key part of the commentary on American politics that both games engage in. According to the canonical version of events established in *Fallout 2*, at some point during the events of *Fallout 1* the Khans abducted Tandi, the daughter of Shady Sands leader, Aradesh. The Vault Dweller, as the player character of *Fallout 1* is referred to in later canon, rescued Tandi and slaughtered almost all of the Khans, with only one member escaping. The stability brought on by eliminating the raiders allowed Shady Sands and the rest of the region to prosper, and the result of that stability is seen in *Fallout 2*: Shady Sands becomes the foundation of a large group of communities known as the New California Republic, and Tandi becomes its second president, ruling it until her death.

The Shady Sands storyline described above is a central element of the Fallout world, as it depicts some important moments that seem small but ultimately become some of the most critical events in the setting. The storyline is also an important in terms of illustrating a specific example of how the franchise comments on American politics. On a surface level, the plot seems to be standard video game fare: a small town in a dangerous land needs help that only the player can provide; someone – and of course, it is a young woman – is kidnapped; the player is sent to rescue them; and the player shoots, stabs, or otherwise kills their way through a dangerous location in order to achieve their goals. The implications and results of those actions are very significant, however, and create many parallels with American colonial history. The story of a small frontier town beset by raiders bears obvious similarities to colonialist narratives about the relationship between early colonial American towns and indigenous American settlements, and while the naming of the Khans does not necessarily reference indigenous American culture, their positioning as a dangerous uncivilized other in relationship to the peaceful civilized Shady Sands is certainly suggestive and particularly insidious given the history of both groups. The Khans' presentation as a tribal group is also quite suggestive, and that presentation remains consistent throughout the Fallout games: in fact, future storylines related to the Khans in *Fallout 2* and *Fallout: New Vegas* (2010) consistently reference the events of previous games, and in later sections of this book I will analyze their portrayal as a group that has been continually marginalized and displaced by the expanding New California Republic and their colonialist ambitions.

It is also worth mentioning an important quality of how the Fallout franchise handles canon before continuing to look at this storyline. *Fallout 1*, like most games in the franchise, has a choice-based story that happens within a specific region of the Fallout world and within a certain time frame in the franchise's timeline. The player has a great deal of choice in terms of what happens in many of the game's locations, such that the potential outcomes of events in the game's story are quite numerous. This leads to a challenge for later games, however, because those games occasionally reference the events of a previous game: as such, they establish a canonical version of what happened in that previous game. This situation is particularly common in *Fallout 2*, as the game takes place not far from where *Fallout 1* took place, leading to many situations in which the events of the previous game are referenced. I claim that this tension is a result of a particular player's playthrough of one of the games relying on what Domsch (2019: 105) refers to as a "spatial narrative" in that it focuses on events that happen in particular locations, while the Fallout world as a whole has a "sequence narrative," which plays out over time. Domsch (2019: 105) notes that "*spatial narrative* as a term is suggested as the opposite of *sequence narrative*," which is likely where this tension arises: the sequential narrative of the overall Fallout franchise cannot account for the various forms that the spatial narratives of a player's individual playthrough of a particular game might take. As such, later games like *Fallout 2* instead establish canonical versions of the events of earlier games, suggesting a specific shape for the spatial narratives contained in those games.

The established Fallout canon relating to this storyline reinforces a commentary on American politics even further because it presents a violent version of how the events related to Shady Sands and the Khans played out in *Fallout 1* even though that is not the only way events in the game can happen. *Fallout 1* presents numerous options for resolving the Shady Sands–Khans storyline: killing all of the Khans is an option, but there are several other potential nonviolent approaches as well, including simply purchasing Tandi's freedom from the Khans, intimidating them into letting her go, or even sneaking in and breaking her out. The established canon suggests that the Vault Dweller chose the violent option, however, murdering nearly everyone present and wiping out the Khans as a threat, at least for a time. The situation is reminiscent of a similar critique of American militarism that Keogh (2012: 20) touches on when discussing *Spec Ops:*

The Line (2012), as he discusses a confrontation between American soldiers and enemy militants that ends in violence "at a time when violence might not have been the only way out of the scenario." Of course, unlike that game, *Fallout 1* is a choice-based game and the player does actually have other options for resolving the situation, but I suggest here that the larger Fallout canon forecloses those choices and assumes that most players will likely take a violent approach to the situation. The commentary on American colonial history can be seen not only in the later Fallout games suggesting that the violent version of events is the canonical version, but also through the results of these actions: Shady Sands and the nearby communities prosper and form a new civilization in the wasteland, in effect validating the approach that the Vault Dweller took and suggesting that violently colonizing the wasteland is an appropriate way to rebuild American society. The Khans do survive and appear in future games as well, though their fate in *Fallout 2* is likewise grim, and their most recent appearance in *Fallout: New Vegas* suggests that they are struggling to survive in the face of the New California Republic's colonial expansion into the Nevada area, though I will discuss their appearances in that game in Chapter 3. Looking at how this storyline progresses in *Fallout 2* is important to seeing how the series continued to comment on American politics in that game, however, a topic I turn to in the next section.

Expanding the World of Fallout: The Map and Timeline of *Fallout 2*

Fallout 2 takes place 80 years after *Fallout 1*, with the game's action focusing on the Chosen One, a descendent of Fallout's protagonist, who hails from a village known as Arroyo. The worlds of *Fallout 1* and *Fallout 2* are closely related: Bainbridge (2017: 158) claims that the games "are chained together, having different stories and main characters but sequenced in the same local history" given the fact that the two games take place in a similar region of the world and that *Fallout 2* follows up on many narrative events from *Fallout 1*. While some civilization has begun to form in the wasteland in *Fallout 2*, much of the world remains a desolate apocalyptic wilderness and survival is still a struggle as it was in the first game. That being said, the stability brought to the region by the Vault Dweller's actions, as well as the rise of several regional powers, means that the map of *Fallout 2* is much more heavily populated than that of *Fallout 1*, with numerous settlements dotted across the map. The map of *Fallout 2* also moves north, centering around the remnants of the cities of Reno and San Francisco, both of which are inhabited by fairly sizable populations. Both cities are not ruled by a single faction but instead have various groups jockeying for power, giving the player a chance to influence those situations. Two other large settlements can be found on the map as well, and those cities are run by groups with very different philosophies: Vault City has a high-tech and well-defended safe zone that is only open to the elite, with slums outside the city gates for the lower class, while the New California Republic has a standing police force and military and offers a home to almost all of the wasteland's inhabitants, even housing a reformed Super Mutant. The stability brought to the region also means that numerous smaller towns can be found across the map as well, including the mining towns of Broken Hills and Redding, the farming and trapping communities of Klamath and Modoc, the ghoul town of Gecko, and the Den, a lawless haven of drug and slave trading.

Relations between the two major powers operating openly in the region, New California Republic and Vault City, are not stable in *Fallout 2*: the two are not in direct conflict, but both are attempting to undermine the other's political aims. New California Republic's main goal is expansion throughout the entire region, and while they do not necessarily aim to conquer by force, they do want to annex as many settlements in the region as they can, including Vault City. Vault City's main goal is to remain independent, as they restrict access to the city to only select a few outside of the original inhabitants of the vault who founded the city and their descendants and have little interest in expansion outside of securing the local territory around their city and maintaining a ghetto for the lower-class workers and servants who support the city. New California Republic has secretly acted against Vault City, however, setting up a covert deal with a crime family from New Reno to hire mercenaries to attack Vault City in the hopes of them requesting military aid from the New California Republic. Much like in *Fallout 1*, the player's actions can directly impact the situation, and *Fallout 2* has various endings that portray the results of those actions: in general, Vault City can either remain independent or end up being annexed by the New California Republic. The later Fallout games are unclear about exactly what the canonical outcome of the situation is, with *Fallout: New Vegas* suggesting that Vault City still exists and that it is within the region controlled by the

New California Republic without outright stating that it was annexed. While this situation is not necessarily a direct commentary on American colonialism, it does depict the New California Republic's colonial ambitions, especially since one character affiliated with the group suggests that Vault City is unpopular due to their pacificist stance that clashes with the New California Republic's expansionist aims.

As noted earlier, the depiction of American style colonialism continues in *Fallout 2*, with the game picking up on the conflict between the New California Republic and the Khans. Much like Shady Sands in the first game, the New California Republic in *Fallout 2* struggles with various issues, two of which are related, unbeknownst to them: a group of squatters has set up a shanty town above the nearby Vault 15, and raiders have been harassing merchant caravans in the area and disrupting trade in the New California Republic. Those squatters are secretly allowing the so-called New Khans to hide inside the vault, using it as a base to conduct their raids while providing food to the squatters, though the Khans claim that they are simply engaging in trade themselves and not attacking nearby merchants. Much like the first game, there are various ways to resolve the situation, and later games also provide a canonical version of what happened: the Chosen One wiped out the New Khans entirely, then negotiated a deal between the squatters and the New California Republic that allowed the New California Republic to annex Vault 15. These events obviously mirror the events of *Fallout 1* in many ways and continue its depiction of colonialism: just like in the previous game, the player's character violently drove out the people living in the area, allowing the expanding colonial power to take over the region and bring civilization to the area, though the Chosen One was even more involved than their predecessor considering they negotiated the annexation agreement as well. The New California Republic is also an even more obvious representation of American politics than Shady Sands given that it is almost explicitly modeled on those politics, including having a democratically elected president, a military, and expansionist aims, a role they continue to fulfill in *Fallout: New Vegas*.

While the New California Republic serves as an obvious analog for America in *Fallout 2*, another faction exists in secret: The Enclave, a group which actually is the remains of the United States military and political structure. The group primarily operates behind the scenes, controlling a military base on the land as well as another hidden base at sea. Unlike the New California Republic, the Enclave has little interest in expansion, at least not until the state of the world is more favorable to their aims; however, they also do not aim to simply remain an independent stronghold like Vault City either. The Enclave's goals instead lie in wiping out the majority of the remaining world population: the group believes that anyone outside of the few people still living in vaults is potentially a dangerous mutant who must be exterminated. The end of *Fallout 2*'s story sees the group attempting to release a virus worldwide that they specifically engineered to only kill humans and mutants, leaving plant and animal life unaffected and allowing America to reclaim control of the world unopposed, though *Fallout 3* (2008) reveals that they were canonically foiled by the Chosen One and their allies. The Enclave serves as one of the Fallout franchise's most straightforward commentaries on the dangers of American militarism and colonialism: the fact that they are the direct representatives of the United States government and military and want to eliminate most of the world's population makes that critique obvious. It is also interesting to note that they are one of the few groups depicted in the games as a wholly villainous faction: while the world of Fallout typically relies on shades of grey for its morality and depicts many groups with nuance, the Enclave serves almost entirely as a force of evil in the game world, a role they continue to fulfill when they make their return in *Fallout 3* and which I look at in the next chapter.

Conclusion: The Foundations of a 25-Year Franchise

In this chapter, I have examined the foundations of the Fallout world by looking at *Fallout 1* and *2*: in less than five years, the two games established a strong world that has since survived for over two decades. While many of the specifics of that world came together late in development, Fallout's inspirations had a lasting impact on the design of all games in the franchise, and the series has roots in tabletop gaming, and especially GURPS, that have persisted long past the mechanical changes that might make the newer games seem less connected to that past. This persistence can be seen in many elements of the Fallout world: the fact that the games still use character statistics that have roots in the tabletop GURPS role-playing game is just one example. Another might be the lack of a character class system: even though there have been many Fallout games, the core structure of a classless-, skill- and stat-based system has remained throughout almost all of the franchise's incarnations. Even skills created for the first game are still used in the games today. Overall, the Fallout world's roots in tabletop gaming are a core part of the franchise, and it seems to be most successful when it sticks to those roots.

Another foundational element of the Fallout world is its aesthetics. While I touch on this topic more in depth in the conclusion of this book to examine why Fallout's aesthetic approach has been so successful, it is worth noting here that the franchise's retro futuristic theming has also been a persistent part of the world throughout almost every Fallout game as well. Lafleuriel (2018: 95) argues that "the combination of post-apocalyptic and retro-futuristic styles is clearly the hallmark of Fallout's design." Similarly, Casas-Roma and Arnedo-Moreno (2019: 3) claim that "one of the signature features that sets it apart from other games would probably be its 1950s retrofuturistic vibe." I further suggest that approach has even inspired other games to try similar approaches: *Atom RPG* (2018), a game whose steam page cites the original Fallout games as a direct inspiration (AtomTeam, 2018), uses a similar art style, but one inspired by Soviet futurism rather than American futurism, leading to an aesthetic that is both influenced by Fallout and clearly distinct from it. Overall, the fact that both future Fallout games and even unaffiliated games inspired by Fallout have used the art style established in *Fallout 1* and *Fallout 2* attests to the strength of the Fallout world's visual design.

Finally, commentary and critique of American history, colonialism, and militarism is a core theme of the Fallout world. Both *Fallout 1* and *Fallout 2* depict several instances of factions attempting to expand and spread their political ideology across the wasteland and major narrative events in both games center around the player's involvement in those struggles. The games establish a backstory in which American militarism was a key factor in the destruction of the world and extend that narrative throughout the game worlds. The Enclave in *Fallout 2* even offers a direct portrayal of the remaining American military and government structure, and the fact that they act as the game's final antagonist offers a fairly clear picture of how the Fallout world expects players to see them. These themes continue throughout much of the franchise as well: only the spinoff games consistently have moved away from them, and that factor may contribute to the way many of those games are not considered canonical entries into the Fallout franchise.

Overall, in this chapter I have suggested that tabletop roots, aesthetics, and political critiques are central to Fallout's world. In the next chapter, I extended my analysis to Bethesda's first two Fallout games, *Fallout 3* and *Fallout 4* (2015). *Fallout 3* came out almost 10 years to the day after *Fallout 2*, leading to a significant gap between the two games, and Bethesda's approach to the franchise differed from the one used in the first two games in some major ways, leading to their games being seen as a reinvention and revival of the franchise. That being said, their games were also true to some of the core themes of the Fallout world, and I will therefore look back at some of the elements I discussed here in the next chapter of this book.

References

AtomTeam, 2018. 'ATOM RPG: Post-apocalyptic indie game,' *Steam,* https://store.steampowered.com/app/552620/ATOM_RPG_Postapocalyptic_indie_game/ (accessed on January 30, 2023.

Bainbridge, William Sims. 2017. *Dynamic Secularization: Information Technology and the Tension between Religion and Science.* Cham: Springer International Publishing.

Barton, Matt. 2010. 'Matt Chat 67: Fallout with Tim Cain Pt. 2." *Youtube,* https://www.youtube.com/watch?v=laq9ua5VjTs (accessed January 30, 2023).

Black Isle Studios. 1998. *Fallout 2: A Post Nuclear Role Playing Game.* Interplay Productions.

Cain, Tim. 2012. 'Classic Game Postmortem: Fallout,' *GDCVault.* https://www.gdcvault.com/play/1015843/Classic-Game-Postmortem (accessed January 30, 2023)

Casas-Roma, Joan and Arendo-Moreno, Joan. 2019. 'Categorizing Morality Systems through the lens of Fallout,' in *DiGRA '19 – Proceedings of the 2019 DiGRA International Conference: Game, Play, and the Emerging Ludo-Mix.*

Domsch, Sebastian. 2019. 'Space and Narrative in Computer Games,' in *Ludotopia: Spaces, Places, and Territories in Computer Games,* edited by Espen Aarseth and Stephan Günzel, pp. 103–123. Bielefeld: Transcript.

Dunne, Daniel Joseph. 'Following the Fallout: Narrative Structures in a Videogame Franchise,' Master's Thesis, Swineburn University of Technology, Australia.

Fullerton, Tracey. 2018. *Game Design Workshop: A Playcentric Approach to Creating Innovating Games,* 4th edition. Natick: A K Peters/CRC Press.

Howard, Kenton Taylor. 2019. 'Nonlinear Narrative in *Fallout 2,*' in *One Shot: A Journal of Critical Play and Games,* 1(1).

Interplay Productions. 1997. *Fallout: A Post Nuclear Role Playing Game.* Interplay Productions.

Keogh, Brenden. 2012. *Killing is Harmless*. Marden: Stolen Projects.

Lafleuriel, Erwan. 2018. *Fallout: A Tale of Mutation: Creation – Universe – Decryption*. Toulouse: Third Editions.

McClancy, Kathleen. 2018. 'The Wasteland of the Real: Nostalgia and Simulacra in Fallout,' in *Game Studies*, 18 (2).

Murray, Soraya. 2018. *On Video Games: The Visual Politics of Race, Gender, and Space*. London/New York: I.B. Tauris.

November, Joseph. 2013. 'Fallout and Yesterday's Impossible Tomorrow,' in *Playing with the Past: Digital Games and the Simulation of History,* edited by Andrew B.R. Elliot and Matthew Wilhelm Kapell, pp. 297–312. London: Bloosbury.

Robertson, Benjamin J. 2018. 'History and Timelines,' in *The Routledge Companion to Imaginary Worlds*, edited by Mark J.P. Wolf, pp. 107–114. London: Routledge.

Wolf, Mark J.P. 2017. 'World Design,' in *The Routledge Companion to Imaginary Worlds*, edited by Mark J.P. Wolf, pp. 67–73. London: Routledge.

2 Reviving the World of Fallout

Fallout 3 and *Fallout 4*

In the previous chapter, I discussed *Fallout 1* (1997) and *Fallout 2* (1998), the first two games in the Fallout franchise, which were published by Interplay; both games were also developed by Interplay, with *Fallout 2*'s Black Isle Studios being a division of the company that focused on role-playing games. The franchise then turned to spinoffs, licensing a first to an outside developer and creating a second using an in-house team with almost no connection to the original games; I look at those spinoff games in the next chapter of this book, which examines Fallout spinoff games in general. After some financial difficulties at Interplay the franchise was sold to Bethesda Softworks, an entirely different video game development and publishing company mostly known for creating the popular open-world fantasy series The Elder Scrolls. Since then, Bethesda has essentially acted like what Wolf (2012: 275) refers to as a torchbearer, who "can be granted the right to continue building a world:," though Wolf uses the term to describe situations in which another person continues the work of a deceased author, the term seems applicable here, as Fallout was essentially a "dead" franchise and before the sale to Bethesda there was little likelihood of a new Fallout game, spinoff or otherwise. In this chapter I turn my attention to two of Bethesda's Fallout games: *Fallout 3* (2008) and *Fallout 4* (2015). I first examine the games from the perspective of world design: I analyze how *Fallout 3* represented both a resurrection of the franchise and a reinvention of it, transforming the Fallout games from a primarily 2D turn-based tactical experience into a fully 3D, action-oriented open-world role-playing game. I then look at how *Fallout 4* pushed that reinvention even further, adding in crafting and base-building mechanics that had never been seen in the franchise before. Finally, I examine how each game uses its world map to continue the commentary on American politics and history that

DOI: 10.4324/9781003395744-3

the franchise was known for, with *Fallout 3*'s setting of Washington D.C. and *Fallout 4*'s setting of Boston allowing each game to portray specific notable locations in American culture. Overall, I argue that while some elements of *Fallout 3* and *Fallout 4* represent a significant shift in world design that moved the series away from its tabletop origins, the games also retained much of the cultural commentary that was a core element of the franchise, such that the two games serve as effective extensions of the Fallout world from an aesthetic perspective and complete reimaginings of many of the Fallout world's mechanical elements.

Before looking at Besthesda's games, it is also worth mentioning here that Interplay was working on a version of *Fallout 3* in the early 2000s, though that version would never be released. Pichlmair (2009: 108) refers to it as "the *Fallout 3* that did not happen," while Lafleuriel (2018: 38) notes that financial issues at Interplay and Black Isle's closing "[sounded] the death knell for a planned *Fallout 3,* known by its code name, *Van Buren.*" These events led to the project's cancellation and the eventual sale of the Fallout intellectual property to Bethesda, leading to the version of *Fallout 3* that I discuss in this chapter. While I do not touch on the canceled version of *Fallout 3* much within this book, I will generally refer to it as *Van Buren* when I do, especially if I am also discussing Bethesda's *Fallout 3* in the same section, simply to reduce confusion between the two games. It is also worth noting that *Van Buren* was "quite some way into development" (Lafleuriel, 2018: 38), with an internal technical demo eventually being made available on the Internet. The demo was surprisingly functional, though the actual length of it was relatively short as it was not intended for public release, and it shows that the game would have been another 2D isometric game like *Fallout 1* and *Fallout 2*, meaning that overall it would have resembled the original games much more than Bethesda's *Fallout 3* and would therefore have not been as significant of a shift in direction for the franchise. Quite a bit of information about *Van Buren*'s development has been made publicly available in interviews, fan forums, and other places, and a fair amount is known about what the game's setting, plot, characters, and more would have looked like. Such information is noncanonical, however, as Bethesda's *Fallout 3* is based on an entirely different premise that bears almost no connection to *Van Buren*'s. Some of the ideas for *Van Buren* were used in *Fallout: New Vegas* (2010), a spinoff game created by developers associated with the original two games and which I discuss in the next chapter, but even that game's story differs significantly from *Van Buren*'s, with only small conceptual elements like certain factions remaining the same. Overall, *Van Buren* occupies an interesting space in the Fallout world, almost operating as a kind of "what if?" Fallout game, and I will refer to it where relevant in this book. That being said, in the next section I turn my attention to Bethesda's Fallout games: when compared to *Van Buren*, they represent quite a different approach to the world of Fallout in many ways.

2D to 3D: Bringing a New Dimension to the World of Fallout with *Fallout 3*

While Interplay's originally planned version of *Fallout 3* was going to be an isometric game like most of the previous games in the franchise, Bethesda's *Fallout 3* was a radical reinvention of the Fallout world in many ways. Perhaps the most obvious reinvention can be seen simply by looking at the visual design and perspective of one of the first few games and then *Fallout 3*: in particular, the isometric perspective used in all the previous games contrasts greatly with the first-person/third-person perspective options available in *Fallout 3*. Such a shift in visual design over the course of a long-running video game franchise is not uncommon: Schwingeler (2019: 52) pointed out that "videogame spaces historically developed from being two-dimensional parallel-projections towards being true linear-perspective constructions," and iconic franchises like Super Mario Brothers and The Legend of Zelda have made similar shifts. A screenshot of a town in *Fallout 2* and one in *Fallout 3* (Figures 2.1 and 2.2) makes the difference between the early games and Bethesda's stand out in terms of visuals. As seen in these images, the game world in *Fallout 2* is presented in an overhead view with the player's avatar moving around on a two-dimensional map, while *Fallout 3* allows the player to look through the eyes of their avatar, with the game offering an optional third-person camera perspective as well (Figure 2.3).

Of course, it is worth noting that *Fallout 3* is technically not the first game to use a 3D world: *Fallout: Brotherhood of Steel* (2004) uses 3D models for its characters and environments, but the game is still presented in an isometric perspective and therefore functions much like a 2D game in most other respects. This change in presentation of the game world is quite an experiment, and *Fallout 3*'s shift from a 2D world to a 3D world was a change not only in visual design but also in

Figure 2.1 A town in Fallout 2.

Figure 2.2 A town in Fallout 3.

map design, which I suggest was an even more fundamental change in world design for the franchise.

Though I discuss the specifics of where *Fallout 3* and *Fallout 4* are set in the next section, here I want to highlight an important difference in map design: all the previous games, regardless of their visual design, were essentially broken down into different maps that the player could traverse. In *Fallout 1* and 2 moving between maps works in one of

Figure 2.3 Third-person camera mode in Fallout 3.

two ways: either by transitioning between different 2D maps like the one shown in the image above or using a 2D overworld map to move between locations. *Fallout Tactics* (2001) and *Fallout: Brotherhood of Steel* use more of a mission-based structure that saw the player completing a particular map and then moving on to the next map in the next mission. In contrast, *Fallout 3* uses a fully 3D open-world map, much like many of Bethesda's previous games, such as *The Elder Scrolls IV: Oblivion* (2006): while the player can "fast travel" to instantly return to previously visited locations, the player otherwise travels the map simply by walking to their desired destination. This leads to a more seamless experience than in previous games, where travel across the map was often broken up into different kinds of experiences intended to represent large-scale overland travel and on-foot travel in specific area: travel in *Fallout 3* is only interrupted by the occasional loading screen seen when fast traveling or when entering towns, buildings, and other specific areas (Figure 2.4).

The other most significant shift seen in *Fallout 3* was a change from the turn-based tactical system seen in *Fallout 1* and *2* to a real-time action-oriented game world. Sid Meier (2012), creator of the Civilization video game series, highlights the difference between turn-based games and real-time games, suggesting that such a difference is quite significant: he even argues that a turn-based game and a real-time game should typically be seen as two entirely different

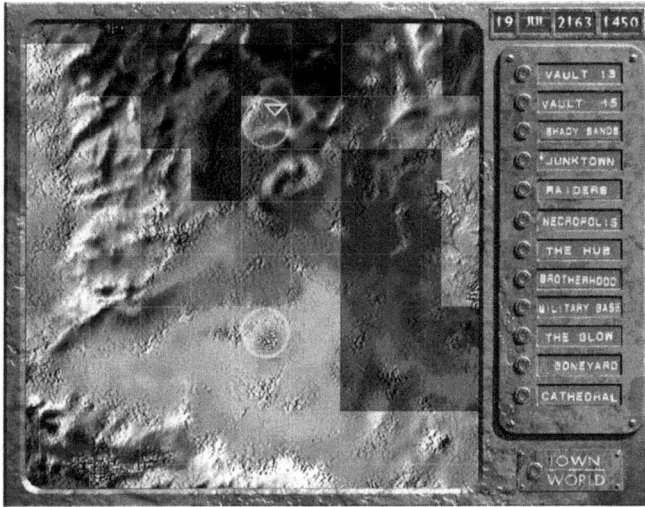

Figure 2.4 Fallout 1 world map.

genres of game. *Fallout 3* was not the first real-time Fallout game, however: experiments with real-time gameplay were attempted in *Fallout Tactics* and *Fallout: Brotherhood of Steel*, with the latter relying on it exclusively. That being said, both of those games are spinoff games and mostly considered noncanonical, so a dramatic change in gameplay is not necessarily surprising: on the other hand, *Fallout 3* is presented as a sequel to the first two games, which might imply that it uses a similar turn-based gameplay structure. Using a real-time approach means that *Fallout 3*'s world is designed much differently than the first two games: one notable example might be how the game worlds are broken down into "hex grids" in the first two games, a structure built around taking turn-based movements on a grid much like in tabletop games. A real-time game needs no such structure, of course, and *Fallout 3*'s world is instead designed like a logical three-dimensional space. As such, I argue that the shift from a turn-based game to a real-time game was not merely a change in genre but also a change in how the world of Fallout is designed at a core level, as well as a move away from a more tabletop gaming inspired experience.

It is also worth noting that beyond the changes in perspective and map design, in general *Fallout 3*'s design more closely resembles the design of Bethesda's previous open-world role-playing game series, The Elder Scrolls, than *Fallout 1* or *Fallout 2*. Bethesda has openly acknowledged the influence of their previous games on *Fallout 3*: Sierra (2020: 24) notes that "the entire team at Bethesda approached the new IP with the intent of keeping their company vales and design vision at the forefront of the new title." *Fallout 3* was therefore in many ways designed to be a Bethesda game first and foremost: the company's goal was not to try to recreate the kind of turn-based iso-metric role-playing game experience found in the first two games. Their desire to acquire the license to make games in the Fallout world was because of its compatibility with Bethesda's world-building phi-losophy, according to a quote from Todd Howard (Bethesda, 2008) in *The Making of Fallout 3*: "We felt in that world, the systems they have in *Fallout 1*, coupled with the way we put things together, we sort of became obsessed: this is the game, we have to make this game." Howard, who has directed all of the Bethesda Fallout games thus far, is also generally known for a focus on world-building in his games, with Sierra (2020: 29) arguing for "the importance he places on game worlds and their design in his games." As such, I suggest the Bethes-da's intention was capturing the aesthetics of the Fallout world rather than attempting a faithful mechanical recreation of it, which to some extent moved the franchise away from its tabletop roots, but did not necessarily impact the elements of political commentary found in the series, a topic I discuss more later on in this chapter.

While the changes in perspective and map design in *Fallout 3* brought the game more in line with other contemporary video games in 2008 and thus increased the popularity of the Fallout franchise, these shifts in world design were not without critique. Lafleuriel (2018: 40) notes that "the concept faced a great deal of mistrust from fans, due to the vast difference between how RPGs like *Elder Scrolls* and *Fallout* worked." As such, "from the initial announcements all the way through to after its release, the game would be burdened with the famous com-parison that '*Fallout 3* is *Oblivion* with guns'" (Lafleuriel, 2018: 40). This fan meme references Bethesda's *The Elder Scrolls IV: Oblivion* and essentially treats *Fallout 3* as if it is an expansion of Bethesda's other popular role-playing game franchise, as those games similarly use 3D open-worlds and have many role-playing elements. The meme has remained popular, with a search for "Oblivion with Guns" on Google returning results on No Mutants Allowed, a popular Fallout fan forum, as well as Reddit, YouTube, GameFAQs, Giant Bomb, and many other video gaming sites. The meme was also responded to by Emil Pagliarulo, a *Fallout 3* writer and developer, who did not necessarily see it as a criticism (Lafleuriel, 2018: 40). This meme does seem to mostly persist in fan spaces, however: though the original article is no longer online, a 2008 review of *Fallout 3* in *PC Gamer Sweden* featured a gaming journalist using the phrase, and that appears to be the only contemporary use of the phrase within mainstream gaming press around the time the game was released (Neoseeker, 2008). Even in such spaces the meme itself is often critiqued: a discussion on the long-running Fallout fans website No Mutants Allowed (norweigan black metal, 2018) forums saw debate about the phrase, with several fans suggesting that it was misguided and perhaps being used by people unfamiliar with the significant differences between the two Bethesda-owned franchises. That forum thread also noted that the phrase had also been applied to *Fallout 4*, Bethesda's follow-up to *Fallout 3*.

While the criticisms of Bethesda's design approach to *Fallout 3* discussed above have been persistent, they did not harm the popularity of their first entry in the Fallout world: *Fallout 3* was quite commercially successful and expanded the popularity of the franchise greatly. Sierra (2020: 22) not only described the first two games as "having a substantial cult following" but also noted that they were "not a blockbuster success," while *Fallout 3* was described as "both a critical and commercial success." Similarly, Lafleuriel (2018: 41) noted that *Fallout 3*'s "commercial success was plain to see, with five million copies sold worldwide and sales that exceeded *Oblivion* in record time." The game's critical success in comparison to *Fallout 1* and *Fallout 2* can also be easily verified by looking at the awards won by the respective games: while *Fallout 1* won a few role-playing game of the year awards and *Fallout 2* was nominated for several, *Fallout 3* won numerous game of the year awards from publications such as IGN, GameSpot, the Golden Joystick awards, and many more. Overall, while there are clear differences in design philosophy between *Fallout 3* and the previous Fallout games, an emphasis on maintaining the consistency of the Fallout world seems to be important to Bethesda. That being said, *Fallout 4* reinvented the franchise even further in terms of world design, which I examine next.

Bringing Civilization to the Wasteland: *Fallout 4*'s Crafting and Settlement Systems

At first glance, *Fallout 4* may not appear to be as radical a reinvention of the Fallout world as the previous game was in terms of world design. A 3D open-world rendition of the franchise was nothing new by the time *Fallout 4* was released in 2015, with the spinoff game *Fallout: New Vegas* being released in the interim and using the same approach that *Fallout 3* did, making *Fallout 4* the third 3D open-world game in the franchise. Bethesda's incredibly popular *The Elder Scrolls V: Skyrim* (2011) also made it clear that the company would continue using the open-world role-playing game approach, so there was no expectation of a return to a 2D isometric world for their next Fallout game. *Fallout 4* therefore retains many of the elements that made *Fallout 3* popular, even returning the series back to the eastern United States after *Fallout: New Vegas*'s brief interlude in the west. The game does reinvent the series in two fairly substantial ways, however, by bring a fully-fledged crafting system to the Fallout world, as well as the ability to build structures, settlements, and effectively even entire towns. The notion of rebuilding and colonizing the wasteland was a narrative element of many previous Fallout games, of course, but I argue here that *Fallout 4* was the first game in which those efforts were something the player could directly engage in themselves through specific mechanics built into the game.

The crafting system in *Fallout 4* is relatively similar to how it is implemented in many other video games, including *The Elder Scrolls V: Skyrim*, though it is quite in-depth compared to many games: nearly any item in *Fallout 4* can be created by the player given the appropriate skills and components. It is also worth noting that some previous Fallout games did have rudimentary crafting systems, with *Fallout: New Vegas*' being the most extensive, though none of the previous games allowed for the crafting of most in-game items as in *Fallout 4*. While crafting could be framed as a system that allows the player to expand the Fallout world, in most cases these crafted items do not have a major impact on the game world, as many of those items consist of weapons, armor, medicine, and other supplies used by the player: the crafting system simply allows players to create such items themselves rather than buying, looting, or otherwise acquiring them. One category of crafted items does have a rather significant impact on the game world and deserves particular attention from a world design perspective, however: settlement items, which are items related to the in-game settlement systems described below. It is also worth mentioning that crafting and world-building systems in games are often linked in such a way: for example, Payne and Huntermann (2019: 5) point out that *Minecraft* (2011) uses a similar approach, with the game's "item-crafting systems [inviting] players to invest countless hours designing their personalized approaches… to designing a sturdy fortress from basic resources." While *Fallout 4*'s crafting system does not have quite as much depth as *Minecraft's* does, settlement items are by far the most numerous, with both defensive structures such as turrets that are aimed at protecting what the player has built and aesthetic items like furniture that are intended to allow the player to personalize their settlements.

The settlement system created for *Fallout 4* is the most revealing mechanic in the franchise in terms of world-building, as it allows the player to participate in world construction quite directly. The system might be compared to the construction systems in games like Minecraft, though Landay (2017: 128) notes that *Minecraft* is an example of an imaginary world in which "storytelling takes a secondary role to world-building," while I would suggest that structure is reversed in *Fallout 4* in that storytelling is still the primary focus. The settlement system effectively allows the player to construct their own towns: certain areas in the game world are designated as potential settlements, and the player can claim those settlements by completing quests in the area that typically involve driving out the local residents, which may consist of radiated monsters and hostile bandits. Another option is working with the Minutemen, a militia group operating in *Fallout 4*'s Commonwealth setting: the group's main goal is establishing defensible settlements in the area, and the Minutemen will help the player take and defend settlements if the player forms an alliance with them. Settlements can consist of buildings, crops, defensive systems, trading posts, and even their own inhabitants, such that the player is able to expand civilization in the region quite significantly. In fact, the player can create far more settlements than there are actual towns in the game: the base game has 30 potential settlement locations, while there are only about 5 towns in *Fallout 4*. Creating settlements is entirely optional, and the player can easily complete the entire game without engaging with the settlement system beyond the tutorials that introduce it, but it is a central part of gameplay in *Fallout 4*. The settlement system also became the foundation for gameplay in Bethesda's next game, *Fallout 76* (2018), which I will discuss more thoroughly in Chapter 4 when I touch on player-created content in the Fallout world.

Fallout 4's crafting and settlement systems should also be considered in light of the series' continual commentary on American colonialism and expansion, as *Fallout 4* might be the game that allows the player to participate in such practices most directly. Previous games certainly implicated the player's choices in regard to those elements – see my discussion of the New California Republic and Khans storylines in Chapters 1 and 3 for more commentary on that subject – but in *Fallout 4* the player can literally bring civilization back to the wasteland, becoming their own colonial power rather than simply enabling the aims of other factions. Murray (2018: 161) suggests that this structure is the case for many game worlds, as they operate as possibility spaces in which "the landscape only fully comes into being as a result of its potential for narrative action, and its capacity to be colonized by a narrative agent," though I claim that *Fallout 4* makes that structure much more literal than most games do, as it is built into the game at a mechanical level. More importantly, this design should also be considered in light of Bethesda's shift towards an open-world game structure for their Fallout games, as Murray (2018: 145) suggests that "open-world games speak to the complexities of power in light of current social and cultural anxieties." How open-world games engage with these complexities varies from game to game, but Murray (2018:145) points out that "the constructions of game landscapes are revelatory in this regard, because they model systems of engagement that betray values, priorities and biases." While *Fallout 3* allows the player to impact the game's landscape in some limited ways, *Fallout 4*'s crafting and settlement systems offer a way for players to imprint their own priorities and biases on the game's landscape quite thoroughly. That being said, the Fallout series has always had a history of engaging with topics like militarism and colonialism, and even without considering the changes the player can make to the game world, the worlds of *Fallout 3* and *Fallout 4* offer plenty to consider in regard to the franchise's commentary on American politics and history, a topic I turn to in the next section of this chapter.

Heading East: The World of Fallout Goes to Washington D.C. and Boston

As noted earlier, while Bethesda's games represent a radical change in world design, they still engage in the same kinds of commentary on American politics and history that the franchise is known for. In the previous chapter I noted that much of that commentary was rooted in the development of a small town, Shady Sands, into a large democratic and expansionist society; that storyline does not continue in Bethesda's games, however, which means that their games must turn to alternate narratives in order to continue the franchise's tradition of commenting on American politics. Rather than relying a storyline centered on the change of a particular region of the world over time, however, *Fallout 3* and *Fallout 4* make such commentary through their settings: *Fallout 3* is set in Washington D.C. and *Fallout 4* is set in Boston. In this section I argue that *Fallout 3* and *Fallout 4* use their maps to portray the dangers of American imperialism by depicting destroyed versions of two iconic American cities, portraying American politics and history through a dark, post-apocalyptic lens.

As noted earlier, *Fallout 3* is set in The Capital Wasteland, the name used for the Washington D.C. area in the Fallout world. Moving to the east coast is quite significant shift in setting from the previous games, most of which took place in the western United States, with *Fallout Tactics* depicting a few locations in the Midwest as well. The game begins with the player leaving their home of Vault 101 in search of their father, who left years ago, and much of the game focuses on exploring the area and looking for clues as to his whereabouts. That search takes the player all over the game world, but especially into the National Mall, an area of D.C. that contains many famous landmarks and monuments, such as the United States Capitol. The player's search is eventually successful, but the player's father is killed when a faction called The Enclave makes an appearance in the region. A water purifier at the Jefferson Memorial that the player's father was working on and the conflict for control of it fills the second half of the game's narrative, with the player eventually being offered the opportunity to complete their father's work and fix the purifier and provide free clean water to the entire region or to instead enact the Enclave's plan of injecting chemicals into the purifier that would taint all the water instead, allowing them to eliminate any mutated creatures in the region. Mukherjee (2019: 168) argues that "the conception of the wasteland has been that of a space without fixed meanings," using *Fallout 3* as an example, but *Fallout 3*'s game world is a space filled with American political monuments. That being said, Mukherjee's description is apt when describing much of The Capital Wasteland, as most of the game's important political locations are found in the National Mall, and much of the rest of the game world consists of a wasteland much like the one found in previous Fallout games. Since *Fallout 3*'s setting contains many locations with political relevance, I do not aim to examine them all in this section; instead, I will highlight a few particular locations that are worth deeper analysis due to their connection with the Fallout world's overall critique of American militarism and colonialism.

As noted above, the Jefferson Memorial is a key location in the story of *Fallout 3*, as the game's plot culminates with a battle for control of the water purifier that has been built at the site. The memorial is certainly notable simply for its connection to the American Revolution, but it becomes transformed into a symbol of militarism throughout the events of the game. At a key moment in the game the Jefferson Memorial is attacked and claimed by the Enclave, a group that represents the remains of the American government and political structure. The final quests of *Fallout 3* see the player staging an assault on the location and reclaiming control of it with the help of the Brotherhood of Steel, an organization with access to advanced technology. Central to the success of the player's mission is Liberty Prime, a giant U.S. military robot that was created during The Great War era to fight against China. Activating the robot allows it to attack the Jefferson Memorial and take down the Enclave's defenses, giving the player a chance to enter and take back control of the location. Liberty Prime's attack on a historic United States monument that is defended by the United States military is a clear instance of irony, one made even more obvious by the over-the-top patriotic voice lines such as "democracy will never be defeated" that the robot shouts while it attacks. The situation is mostly portrayed humorously, but not all of *Fallout 3*'s political commentary has such a light-hearted approach.

Another particularly politically charged location in *Fallout 3* is the United States Capitol, as it is quite literally a central hub of political action in the real world. In *Fallout 3* the Capitol is the site of a massive battle between a mercenary group named Talon Company and a group of Super Mutants, a conflict that the player essentially gets caught in the middle of upon reaching the area. As the game progresses another group enters the fray: The Enclave eventually sets up camp near the Capitol in their own attempt to control the area. This situation intensifies the dimension of the political commentary seen in previous games that present the Enclave as an enemy: while the player invades an Enclave base during the conclusion of *Fallout 2* as I discussed in the previous chapter, in *Fallout 3* the player can literally do battle with the remains of the United States military on the steps of the Capitol building. The Enclave will even carpet bomb the area with mini nukes using a helicopter if the player approaches the area from a certain position, leading to a situation in which mushroom clouds that were created by the United States government can be seen floating over one of the most important locations in its own country's politics. While the in-game location can certainly be seen as in line with the Fallout franchise's critique of American militarism, it also has a literal connection to it: *Fallout 3* concept art depicting the destroyed United States Capitol was included in a video that was posted on suspected terrorist websites, and a United States military contractor labeled the image as potentially being created by Al-Qaeda (Thompson, 2008). Even more interestingly, events since the game's release have also cast the game's portrayal of the United States Capitol in a different light, and the situation now recalls Murray's (2018: 151) discussion of *Metal Gear Solid V: The Phantom Pain* (2015): she commented that "the highly mediated space of the game simulates particular ideas about a lived place, even while it traffics in ideology" in reference to that game's depiction of 1980s Afghanistan. Of course, *Fallout 3* setting such a violent battle inside one of the most important government buildings in the United States was already a form of trafficking in ideology when the game was released in 2008, but that battle takes on a new light in the aftermath of the Capitol Riots of 2021, as seeing a bloody conflict taking place inside the Capitol is now something that is a part of people's actual lived experience. As such, the ideological elements of *Fallout 3*'s depiction of the United States Capitol might be interpreted entirely differently than how they were originally intended.

Finally, one location worth looking at in *Fallout 3* is the Lincoln Memorial, though it is connected more to the Fallout world's critique of American history and society rather than its themes of militarism. It is worth noting here that slavery shows up frequently in the Fallout world: *Fallout 2* and *Fallout: New Vegas* both depict it explicitly, as does *Fallout 4*. *Fallout 3* might offer the most direct commentary on it, however, by featuring slavery as a central element of a quest set at the Lincoln Memorial called "Head of State." When the player finds the Lincoln Memorial in *Fallout 3* it has been overrun by a faction of slavers from the nearby Paradise Falls. The group is considering destroying the location entirely, and the head of Lincoln's statue is already missing. The player can be sent to the location on the "Head of State" quest by a group of abolitionists with the goal of finding the missing statue head and driving out the slavers; the player can do so or can side with the slavers instead, helping them wipe out the abolitionists. The story surrounding the Lincoln Memorial in *Fallout 3* is therefore quite clear about its commentary on American history in offering the player a direct choice in siding with abolitionists or slavers, but perhaps even more interesting is that the game even foregrounds the ideological elements of its commentary: the slavers explicitly mention that they want to control and destroy the Lincoln Memorial to wipe out the memory of abolitionism in the United States. It is also worth noting that the game itself poses an ethical commentary on these events: like other games in the series, the game has a karma system that tracks some in game actions, providing positive karma is the action if it is considered good and negative karma if it is consider evil. Karma is a significant part of the game: Sicart (2013: 96) points out that "many actions in the game, from stealing to freeing slaves, are awarded with karma points," and Schulzke (2009) claims that while "moral choice is a part of many video games, especially RPGs... the *Fallout* series and especially *Fallout 3* have taken it to a new level." "Head of State" is explicitly tracked using the karma system and is even potentially tied to the game's ending, as siding with the slavers awards a large amount of negative karma, while restoring the monument and then finishing the game with a good overall karma score provide a special ending video that depicts the restored memorial. While the game ties this commentary on American history to morality, this more history-focused narrative also perhaps foreshadowed the approach Bethesda would take in *Fallout 4*, which I look at more in depth below.

While the player's journey starts inside a vault in *Fallout 4*, much like many of the previous games, the circumstances are quite different: the player, along with their spouse and son, was cryogenically frozen on the day of The Great War. The game begins with a mysterious figure murdering the player's spouse and kidnapping their son, and much of the game's plot revolves around tracking down that figure and eventually find the said son. The player's son turns out to be the leader of The Institute, one of The Commonwealth's most powerful factions, who reside inside the remains of the Massachusetts Institute of Technology. The latter half of the game sees the player siding with either The Institute or one of the three other major factions in the area, all of whom have different goals for the region. Siding with some factions requires the elimination of others, making certain choices mutually exclusive and locking the player out of some potential quests and storylines, though the specifics of each situation depends on the factions themselves. One option is The Railroad, a group whose goals are diametrically opposed to The Institute, as they aim to free the Synths, who are intelligent humanoid android servants created by The Institute. The Minutemen are another more neutral option, with their goal simply being to establish defensible settlements in the area and protect the people who live in them. The Brotherhood of Steel are the final option, who have similar aims to the role in previous games: maintaining control of powerful pre-war technology. The choice of which faction to side with also significantly impacts the game world of *Fallout 4*, as after the game is completed the player can continue exploring the wasteland and the faction the player sided with will have control of the region.

Like the previous game, *Fallout 4*'s map features many real-world locations, though they are perhaps less overtly politically charged than *Fallout 3*'s simply due to the change in setting from Washington D.C. to Boston. That being said, many of the locations in the game are tied to specific historical events, such that *Fallout 4*'s map comments on American history in ways that fit very well with the franchise's overall commentary on American society. Perhaps the most overt of these is *Fallout 4*'s Museum of Witchcraft, an in-game location that directly corresponds with the real-life Salem Witch Museum. The in-game location contains computer terminals that refer to exhibits in the real-life museum, though the location has been mostly destroyed and is overrun with monsters by the time the player visits it in *Fallout 4*. The historical persecution of witches is also used as a mirror for the in-game plotline surrounding Synths, synthetically created humanoid robots made by the Institute, who are feared among the population of The Commonwealth.

Another location that directly corresponds to a real-world location is The Institute, a hidden stronghold for the faction of the same name. The Institute is built underground beneath the ruins of the Commonwealth Institute of Technology, or C.I.T., an analog for the real-world Massachusetts Institute of Technology. The location and faction were both founded by survivors of The Great War, who used their scientific knowledge and the technology available to them to build underground facilities. By the time of *Fallout 4* the location is massive, roughly the size and structure of an actual college, and features specialized facilities for various scientific pursuits, such as bioscience and robotics. While The Institute may seem to simply be a benign, futuristic version of the real-life location, it is worth noting that they are perhaps the most overtly evil faction depicted in *Fallout 4*: they created the Synths to act on their own goals in the Commonwealth and essentially treat them as disposable servants. The situation may not seem morally questionable at first, but exploring the Institute's history reveals that while the Synths began as fully robotic beings with simple programmed AIs, by the time of *Fallout 4* the Institute has created "Third Generation" Synths that are created from organic material based on DNA provided by the Institute's founder. These third-generation Synths are fully sentient and biological, though they have some technological implants, most notably a brain implant that allows them to be controlled via vocal commands. Many third-generation Synths even attempt to break free of the Institute entirely, necessitating the creation of an internal "Synth Retention Bureau" that hunts down escaped Synths. The Institute is feared throughout the Commonwealth for many reasons, including their practice of kidnapping humans for experimentation and replacing them with Synths, and therefore keeps their location and presence a secret as much as possible. As such, *Fallout 4* could be seen as offering a critique of American scientific positivism, which often sees science as a solution rather than a problem. Such a critique would certainly not be out of place in a series set in a post-nuclear apocalyptic wasteland since it is already an inherent part of the franchise, but connecting that critique to such a specific real-world location certainly casts it in a different light.

It is also worth noting that some of *Fallout 4*'s factions are also designed to mirror real-world groups from American history, providing further commentary on that history. The Minutemen are likely the first example that the player will encounter, as they are tied to the settlement system that is quite prominent in *Fallout 4*. The Minutemen aim to bring civilization back to the Wasteland much like the New California Republic of the previous games, though they are significantly less organized and operate more like a militia rather than a functioning colonial government. The other most significant such group is The Railroad, a faction dedicated to helping Synths escape from their Institute masters and attempting to integrate them into society. The storyline is a quite obvious parallel for the real-life Underground Railroad, with The Railroad portraying the third-generation Synths as living slaves whom the Institute treats like property rather than sentient beings, though not all in the region agree with that sentiment: The Brotherhood of Steel, for example, views Synths as a menace that needs to be wiped out. As mentioned earlier, the game's main quest allows the player to side with The Minutemen or The Railroad as well as The Institute, giving the player an opportunity to involve themselves directly in the situation, and siding with a particular group leads to them achieving their goals and making their mark on The Commonwealth. As such, the game's main quest essentially asks the player to make an ideological choice about which group might be best suited to control the area, mirroring similar decisions in previous Fallout games in a way that is in line with the Fallout world's overall aesthetic.

Conclusion: Reinventing the World of Fallout

This chapter has focused on Bethesda's reinvention of the world of Fallout: while the games began as 2D isometric games with clear roots in tabletop role-playing games, Bethesda expanded both the way the franchise is structured and the popularity of the series. As they are currently the rights holders of the Fallout franchise, their approach to the world of Fallout is likely to be the dominant one for the foreseeable future. While Bethesda's games have been criticized due to the company changing some of the core elements of the Fallout experience, their success on both commercial and critical fronts suggests that their changes have not been unwelcome. Furthermore, in this chapter I have argued that Bethesda's Fallout games are in line with the overall aesthetics of the world: they retain the retro futuristic visual design that I touched on in Chapter 1, but more importantly they also maintain the Fallout world's critique of American politics, a critique which is central to the mood and feel of Fallout. As such, I suggest that Bethesda's games should be seen as legitimate entries in the Fallout franchise regardless of those games being created by an entirely different developer nearly ten years after *Fallout 1* and *Fallout 2* were released and that they established a logic of reinvention within the Fallout franchise, a concept I explore further in the next chapter while looking at the various Fallout spinoff games.

While I mentioned some of the critiques of the Bethesda games earlier in this chapter, it is also worth addressing the mechanical changes to the Fallout world that Bethesda made with *Fallout 3* and *Fallout 4*. These changes could be legitimately critiqued from the perspective of world design since they mostly move the Fallout world away from its tabletop gaming roots, but it is also worth noting that those changes are in line with overall trends in the video game industry, as turn-based tactical role-playing games with a clear tabletop gaming influence are not nearly as popular as they were in the 1990s when *Fallout 1* and *Fallout 2* were released. In fact, it is worth pointing out that experiments with these game mechanics began well before Bethesda: as I touch on in the next chapter, *Fallout Tactics* and *Fallout: Brotherhood of Steel* were both spinoff games released in the interim between *Fallout 2* and *Fallout 3* and had real-time gameplay. While elements of those games are not considered part of the Fallout canon, they both demonstrate that experimentation with mechanics was a part of the Fallout world well before Bethesda took over the franchise.

Overall, this chapter has examined Bethesda's entries in the Fallout universe to look at how the company both reinvented the franchise and expanded its canon beyond the stories told in the first two Fallout games. The next chapter expands that analysis to look at Fallout spinoff games: the series has had at least four spinoff games, though what exactly counts as a Fallout spinoff could certainly be debated. Those games also expand Fallout's gameplay well beyond the real-time action open-world role-playing game structure used by Bethesda, though one of them, *Fallout: New Vegas*, actually uses the game engine and many of the same assets as *Fallout 3*. As such, looking at the ways in which the Fallout world has been spun off into various forms is this book's next focus, and I turn to that notion in the next chapter.

References

Bethesda Game Studios. 2008a. *Fallout 3*. Bethesda Softworks.

Bethesda Game Studios. 2008b. *The Making of Fallout 3* [bonus disc included with *Fallout 3* collector's edition]. Bethesda Softworks.

Black Isle Studios. 1998. *Fallout 2: A Post Nuclear Role Playing Game*. Interplay Productions.

Interplay Productions. 1997. *Fallout: A Post Nuclear Role Playing Game*. Interplay Productions.

Lafleuriel, Erwan. 2018. *Fallout: A Tale of Mutation: Creation – Universe – Decryption*. Toulouse: Third Editions.

Landay, Lori. 2013. 'Minecraft: Transnational Objects and Transformational Experiences in an Imaginary World,' in *Revisiting Imaginary Worlds: A Subcreation Studies Anthology*, edited by Mark J.P. Wolf, pp. 127–148. London: Routledge.

Meier, Sid. 2012. 'Interesting Decisions," *GDC Vault.* https://www.gdcvault.com/play/1015756/Interesting (accessed January 30, 2023).

Mukerjee, Souvik. 2019. 'Video Game Wastelands as (Non-)Places and "Any Space Whatevers",' in *Ludotopia: Spaces, Places, and Territories in Computer Games,* edited by Espen Aarseth and Stephan Günzel, pp. 167–184. Bielefeld: Transcript.

Murray, Soraya. 2018. *On Video Games: The Visual Politics of Race, Gender, and Space.* London/New York: I.B. Tauris.

norweigan black metal. 2018. 'Why is *Fallout 3* called "Oblivion With Guns?",' *No Mutants Allowed* (February 24). https://www.nma-fallout.com/threads/why-is-fallout-3-called- oblivion-with-guns.215266/ (accessed January 30, 2023).

Payne, Matthew Thomas and Huntermann. Nina (eds.) 2019. *How to Play Video Games.* New York: NYU Press.

Pichlmar, Martin. 2019. 'Assembling a Mosaic of the Future: The Post-Nuclear World of Fallout 3,' in *Eludamos: Journal for Computer Game Culture* 3(1), pp. 107–113.

Schwingeler, Stephan. 2019. 'Playing with Sight: Construction of Perspective in Videogames,' in *Ludotopia: Spaces, Places, and Territories in Computer Games,* edited by Espen Aarseth and Stephan Günzel, pp. 41–60. Bielefeld: Transcript.

Schulzke, Marcus. 2009. 'Moral Decision Making in Fallout,' in *Game Studies* 9(2).

Sicart, Miguel. 2013. *Beyond Choices: The Design of Ethical Gameplay.* Cambridge: The MIT Press.

Sierra, Wendy. 2020. *Todd Howard: Worldbuilding in Tamriel and Beyond (Influential Game Designers).* London: Bloomsbury Academic.

Spiess, Kevin. 2008. 'Swedish Review: *Fallout 3* 'Oblivion with Guns', Gives Game a 81%," *Neoseeker* (October 8). https://www.neoseeker.com/news/8987-swedish-reviewer-fallout-3- oblivion-with-guns-gives-game-a-81/} (accessed January 30, 2023).

Thompson, Michael. 2008. '*Fallout 3* Screen Mistaken for Al Qaeda Image,' *Ars Technica,* (June 2). https://arstechnica.com/gaming/2008/06/fallout-3-screen-mistaken-for-al-qaeda- image/ (accessed January 30, 2023).

Wolf, Mark J. P. 2012. *Building Imaginary Worlds: The Theory and History of Subcreation.* London: Routledge.

3 Expanding the World of Fallout

Fallout Spinoff Games

The world of Fallout is quite expansive, and in the previous two chapters of this book I looked at the four main Fallout games: *Fallout 1* (1997), *Fallout 2* (1998), *Fallout 3* (2018), and *Fallout 4* (2015) comprise the core single player role-playing game experience of the Fallout world in the eyes of most fans. In this chapter I expand my scope to examine the various Fallout spinoff games, of which there are also four: *Fallout Tactics: Brotherhood of Steel* (2001), which I will refer to throughout this chapter simply as *Fallout Tactics* to differentiate it from *Fallout: Brotherhood of Steel* (2004), an entirely different spinoff game, as well as *Fallout Shelter* (2015) and *Fallout: New Vegas* (2010). Fallout Pinball, an expansion pack for *Bethesda Pinball* (2016) could also potentially be considered a fifth spinoff game, though I will exclude it from this analysis as it is a Fallout-themed pinball game: it has little connection to the world of Fallout beyond that theming, and I instead touch on it a bit in the concluding chapter where I discuss Fallout's forays into other forms of media. *Fallout 76* (2018) could also debatably be considered a spinoff game, but I exclude it from this chapter for two reasons: one is simply because Bethesda presents it as a prequel to the main Fallout series, and the other is because the great deal of player-created content in the game causes it to fit well with other player-created content like mods and tabletop campaigns that I discuss in Chapter 4. *Fallout: New Vegas* is also often considered a main Fallout game rather than a spinoff since it functions much like a sequel to the first two games, but I discuss it in this chapter due to its relationship to the Fallout canon in comparison to other Fallout spinoffs.

The main focus of my analysis of the Fallout spinoff games in this chapter is related to canonicity, as one of the primary distinguishing factors between the main Fallout games and Fallout spinoff games

DOI: 10.4324/9781003395744-4

is whether or not they are considered canonical, with *Fallout: New Vegas* being the only canonical spinoff game. Wolf (2012: 270–271) discusses the notion of varying levels of canonicity, outlining numerous considerations related to how a particular work might be considered canon. He notes that "some worlds have very well-defined levels of canonicity" (Wolf, 2012: 271) and cites the Star Wars franchise as a notable example, a comparison that is quite useful when looking at similar situations in the Fallout franchise. In comparison to Star Wars, the Fallout world has less-defined levels of canonicity, and Fallout spinoff games in particular vary quite a bit in terms of whether their events are considered canon – and even what considerations should go into such decisions. As a brief summary of the situation, two of those games, *Fallout Tactics* and *Fallout: Brotherhood of Steel*, are mostly considered noncanonical by both the current creators of the franchise and most fans. Bethesda's *Fallout Shelter* has an interesting relationship to the Fallout canon: the in-game events are not presented as canonical, and indeed many of them can actually violate the Fallout canon in extreme ways, but the game itself does not have a specific plot and is instead presented almost as if it is a simulation of Fallout's in-universe vaults. Finally, *Fallout: New Vegas* was created by Obsidian Entertainment, a developer with ties to Interplay and Black Isle, the developers of the first two games, which may be why it is the only Fallout spinoff game that is considered fully canonical. This situation is reminiscent of how canonicity in many franchises with multiple different creators works, as when discussing the Star Wars franchise and its various tie-in and spinoff novels, Proctor and Freeman (2017: 226–227) pointed out that "terms such as 'tie-ins,' 'spin offs' and 'franchise novels' are freighted with cultural value: they 'tie in' with a 'master-narrative' text, or 'spin off ' from it, like a naughty child disobeying the authority of the parent." Overall, in this chapter I argue that one of the most unique elements of the Fallout world is its canon: the world has been expanded in many ways, and those expansions come with varying degrees of success in terms of whether or not they are considered faithful to the canon of the Fallout world.

Before continuing to look at the Fallout spinoffs in relationship to canonicity, it is also noting that Bethesda Softworks, the current rights holders and developers of the Fallout intellectual property, are not the original creators of the franchise. I discussed Bethesda's revival of the series in the previous chapter in the context of the design changes they made and the reactions fans and journalists had to those changes, but since this chapter discusses canonicity it is worth briefly addressing the notion of canonicity in relationship to the Bethesda Fallout games. While Bethesda is currently the arbiter of the Fallout world's canon from an authorial perspective, canon operates on multiple levels, and Wolf (2012: 271) points out that fans often make their own determinations related to canon as well: "just as there are circles of authorship, there are circles of canonicity, and purists may accept less material as canonical than will a casual audience member." This statement certainly applies to the Fallout fan base, in which there are purist segments of the Fallout fan community who do not consider any games created after *Fallout 2* part of the Fallout canon, with *Fallout: New Vegas* being the only potential exception. Such fans view games like *Fallout 3*, *Fallout 4*, and *Fallout 76* as noncanonical alongside many of the spinoff games. This situation hotly debated, however, and is again reminiscent of a similar situation in the Star Wars franchise: as Proctor and Freeman (2017: 228) note, debates about whether or not material in the Star Wars novels are considered canon results in what fans call "canon wars." Proctor and Freeman (2017: 228) describe the situation like this: "as fans struggle to maintain their individual viewpoints, 'canon wars' of this kind provide a space whereby textual expertise is marshalled as a form of competition." A similar situation in the case of the Fallout franchise simply replaces the said textual expertise with game expertise and knowledge and knowledge of the franchise's history with purist fans especially emphasizing knowledge of the older games as a kind of marker of expertise in the Fallout world. That being said, as noted in Chapter 2, Bethesda's games brought a great deal more popularity and attention to the franchise, and the notion that their games are not part of the Fallout canon is relatively small within the overall Fallout fanbase. I do not intend to engage in a lengthy discussion of that notion here since I also touched on fan criticisms of Bethesda's Fallout games in the previous chapter, but it is worth noting that this book treats the Bethesda Fallout games as part of the Fallout canon and that it generally aligns with their position on the canonicity of the Fallout spinoffs, in particular with regard to the canonicity of *Fallout Tactics* and *Fallout: Brotherhood of Steel*. I take this position simply because Bethesda is the current rights holder of the franchise: while fan responses to their games may vary, any future expansions of the Fallout world for the foreseeable future will likely be overseen by Bethesda from an authorial perspective.

In terms of structure, this chapter first examines the canonicity of *Fallout Tactics* and then *Fallout: Brotherhood of Steel*: most of the events of the former game are not considered canon, and all of the events of the latter are not. I then examine the canonicity of *Fallout Shelter*, as it resides in a state of what I call *metacanonicity* in that it references events from throughout the Fallout canon while operating both within and outside of that canon. Finally, my analysis of canonicity in this chapter turns to *Fallout: New Vegas*, the only Fallout spinoff game that is fully canonical. Overall, I argue that the Fallout franchise is designed to be redesigned, even if all of those experiments with world-building are not always successful: debates about canonicity began early in the franchise's history and have continued throughout it, establishing a logic of reinvention that various game developers have used to put their own mark on the world of Fallout and a logic that extends to the fan creations, mods, and tabletop campaigns that I discuss in the next chapter.

Semi-canonicity: *Fallout Tactics*

Fallout Tactics was the first Fallout spinoff game: the first two games were relatively successful, leading to desire from many for a follow-up game. I touched on the cancelled *Fallout 3* project created by Interplay in the previous chapter, which was code named *Van Buren* and which I will refer to it as in this chapter to distinguish it from Bethesda's *Fallout 3*; Interplay was working on that project after *Fallout 2*, but the company decided that spinoff games might be the best way to fill the gap until the game's release, as the first two games came out within a year of each other and *Van Buren* was slated for several years after that. *Fallout Tactics* was created by Micro Forte, an Australian game development company that tended to work with larger American publishers by creating new games within established franchises; before working with Interplay they created several games for Electronic Arts. In general, during this time Micro Forte acted much like what Wolf (2012: 276) refers to as an employee or freelancer in that they were "unable to initiate new works, perform retconning, or add new canonical material without permission from the author… they [were] hired hands who [were] assigned tasks and paid for them." McCrea (2013: 203) notes that this situation was common in the Australian video game industry at the time, claiming that "this model became known internationally as the work-for-hire model, among other less generous names" and that it often made it difficult for companies like Micro Forte to remain profitable. The core of the game was originally not based on Fallout at all, as Micro Forte had created the framework for a tactical combat game but not a specific story or setting; however, Interplay suggested setting the game in the Fallout world. There was also some connection between the first two Fallout games and those who worked on *Fallout Tactics*: Chris Taylor, who worked on *Fallout 1* and was likely the most influential person on the game's development other than Tim Cain, was the lead designer for *Fallout Tactics*. Overall, however, *Fallout Tactics* was envisioned as a move in a different direction for the Fallout franchise using a different development approach than the first two games used.

Fallout Tactics was also not intended to be a significant narrative expansion to the Fallout world. Lafleuriel (2018: 53) notes that "it is not an RPG in a traditional sense, because the story is limited to a series of confrontations in which players fight to get out alive." It also moved away from being choice-based, as Schulzke (2009) claims that

> with the exception of the series' tactical RPG, *Fallout Tactics,* the games allow for a great deal of personal choice including what quests to complete, how to complete them, what kind of character to create, and how to explore the map.

That being said, outsourcing the game's development meant that the team that created was not the same, and the team made some very deliberate moves away from the gameplay of *Fallout 1* and *Fallout 2*: A CNET Gamecenter preview article from September 2000, a few months before the game's release, highlighting the change and noting that "Interplay thinks it's time for a change. The publisher has snatched a page from SquareSoft's playbook, and is looking to focus almost entirely on the action elements of this successful RPG franchise" (Walker, 2000). The reference to "SquareSoft's playbook" is a nod to the game's name and inspiration, which Chris Taylor commented on in the article: "Final Fantasy Tactics (FFT) was an obvious influence… besides the name similarities, we looked at how they converted an RPG into a tactical combat game" (Walker, 2000). Overall, *Fallout Tactics* was an expansion of the Fallout world by a new developer and was also an attempt to reinvent the franchise by moving away from a more narrative-focused game and towards one more based on action, establishing a logic of reinvention within the Fallout world that would later be used by Bethesda to revive the franchise for their version of *Fallout 3*.

At the time it was released, canonicity was not an issue for *Fallout Tactics*, and there was little discussion about whether or not the events and elements of the Fallout world depicted in the game would be considered canonical for *Van Buren*. From a narrative perspective the game might be considered less "story heavy" because of its focus on tactical combat, but it did introduce some new elements to the Fallout world. That being said, *Fallout Tactics* focused less on political commentary than the previous games did, which can be seen in a summary of the game's story: it focuses on working with a splinter group of the Brotherhood of Steel, a faction in the wasteland that aims to reclaim old world technology, rather than navigating the conflicts between various different politically oriented factions like the first two games did. The group was important in the first two games, but *Fallout Tactics* was the first game in the franchise to focus entirely on the faction: the player starts out as a member of the Brotherhood of Steel and works to further their aims throughout the entire game. The game takes place in Chicago, a yet unexplored part of the Fallout world, but portions of the game also spill over into Missouri, especially St. Louis and Kansas City, and eventually to Vault Zero, a hidden vault in the Cheyenne Mountain, Colorado region. Battles with raiders, mutants, and a robot army make up the bulk of the game's story, which ends with the Brotherhood of Steel locating the robot army's leader, The Calculator, hidden in Vault Zero, and finding some way to stop the advances of the robots. Overall, the game's narrative is more straightforward and less driven by player choice and faction struggles than the previous two Fallout games, but on the surface, it does not appear to be inconsistent with elements from *Fallout 1* and *Fallout 2*: it simply seems less in line with the kind of themes and political commentary that the previous games were known for.

Issues with canonicity and *Fallout Tactics* arose when Bethesda begins planning to create their own version of *Fallout 3*: since *Fallout 3* was obviously intended to be a sequel to the first two games and was going to show players a new expansion of the Fallout world the events of the previous games had to be accounted for. Bethesda's approach to the first two games was fairly straightforward: much like *Fallout 2* did with the events of *Fallout 1*, Bethesda decided that *Fallout 3* would reference those events at times, and when necessary the game mentions canonical versions of what happened in previous games. Challenges arose with *Fallout Tactics*, however, because of its focus on the Brotherhood of Steel: *Fallout 3*'s plot similarly relies on a splinter group of the Brotherhood of Steel, which immediately begged questions about whether the group was the same group depicted in *Fallout Tactics* or at least what their relationship to the group from *Fallout Tactics* was. During the development of *Fallout 3* it seemed that Bethesda would simply ignore the events of *Fallout Tactics* entirely: in a 2007 *Gamespy* interview over a year before the game was released, for example, *Fallout 3*'s executive producer, Todd Howard, commented that "for our purposes, neither *Fallout Tactics* nor *Fallout: Brotherhood of Steel* happened" (Nguyen, 2007). This stance seemed to change slightly over time, however, and Lafleuriel (2018: 54) claims that "its content was classed as canon by Bethesda since it acquired the license." Bethesda now sells the game themselves and has a page for *Fallout Tactics* on their own website, where they have a description of the game:

> In these dark times, the Brotherhood of Steel is all that stands between the rekindled flame of civilization and the radiated Wasteland. Take up arms, stand shoulder to shoulder with your brethren, and protect the weak, whether they like it or not. Your squadmates will be more dear to you than family and for those that survive there will be honor, respect and the spoils of war.

(Bethesda.net)

There are also a few references to *Fallout Tactics* in later Fallout games, though they are relatively minor. One of those references comes in *Fallout 3* itself, with a Brotherhood of Steel member commenting that there is "a small detachment in Chicago, but they're off the radar. Gone rogue. Long story" (Bethesda Softworks, 2008). *Fallout: New Vegas* also contains a small reference to *Fallout Tactics* with a character mentioning an encounter with the "Brotherhood of Steel in Colorado," suggesting that perhaps the group stayed active in the region after the events of *Fallout Tactics* (Obsidian Entertainment, 2010). That being said, the general consensus among both developers and fans is that at much of the game is semi-canonical at best, and likewise *Fallout Tactics'* status within the overall Fallout world's canon is questionable as well, though it still seems to enjoy a bit more of a canonical status than the next Fallout spinoff game, *Fallout: Brotherhood of Steel*, which I discuss in the next section.

Noncanonicity: *Fallout: Brotherhood of Steel*

Like its predecessor *Fallout Tactics*, *Fallout: Brotherhood of Steel* was another significant shift in terms of gameplay for the Fallout world: it dropped the grid-based tactical combat of previous games entirely in favor of a 3D isometric "arcade" style action game. Lafleuriel (2018: 55) described the game as "a vaguely RPG-like action game that incorporates some elements of the *Fallout* saga, but runs roughshod over the rest," with the game's narrative elements in particular being a common sticking point for most Fallout fans as many of them are inconsistent with established details of the Fallout world. As a brief summary, the game's plot takes place between the events of *Fallout 1* and *Fallout 2* and centers around the town of Carbon in post-apocalyptic Texas. The game differs from previous Fallout games in that the player takes on the role of specific characters throughout the game's story, most of whom are members of the Brotherhood of Steel. Much of the game's events revolve around the Brotherhood's battle against a group of Super Mutants, and as the game progresses it is revealed that those mutants have found a way to reproduce naturally instead of using their previous methods, which involved capturing radiation-free humans and "dipping" them in a chemical that turns them into mutants. The game's plot features appearances from characters from previous games, most notably The Vault Dweller, *Fallout 1*'s protagonist, and Harold, a ghoul-like character who makes appearances in *Fallout 1*, *Fallout 2*, and *Fallout 3*. From a plot perspective, one reason why the events of *Fallout: Brotherhood of Steel* might be considered an issue is simply because of the appearance of these two characters: they are not relatively minor side characters that could appear in a spinoff game without any consequences for the overall Fallout canon, as both play extremely significant roles in the Fallout world. The characters also play fairly significant roles in *Fallout: Brotherhood of Steel*, with the Vault Dweller even becoming a playable character after completing the game up to a certain point. The game's storyline is also a bit inconsistent with details established in *Fallout 2*, even though *Fallout: Brotherhood of Steel* is supposed to take place before *Fallout 2*. Of course, Lessa and Araujo (2017: 91) note that "despite the efforts of many authors and fans to avoid or explain away inconsistencies, irreducibly contradictory fictional worlds abound in any medium," and there are many examples of entries into imaginary worlds that introduced elements that were wholly inconsistent with the rest of that world's logic;

Fallout: Brotherhood of Steel could simply be seen as another entry on that list. That being said, as shown in the previous section, *Fallout Tactics* already had its own issues with canonicity that Bethesda had to address when developing *Fallout 3*, and *Fallout: Brotherhood of Steel* inconsistencies were much more significant than the ones found in that game. As such, it may have just been simpler for Bethesda to declare the game's events entirely noncanonical, as otherwise *Fallout 3* would have needed to account for them, especially since the Brotherhood of Steel, Super Mutants, and Harold all make prominent appearances in *Fallout 3* as well.

Another commonly cited issue with *Fallout: Brotherhood of Steel* is the game's aesthetics and tone, which many feel clash greatly with the rest of the established Fallout world. While the game's visuals are usually not too heavily criticized as they still draw inspiration from previous Fallout games, the most commonly cited complaint related to the game's aesthetics is likely its musical direction. The previous Fallout games primarily featured low-key ambient music during game-play, and the introductory videos for *Fallout 1* and 2 featured classic 1940s and 1950s tracks: *Fallout 1* used The Ink Spots' performance of "Maybe," while *Fallout 2* used Louis Armstrong's interpretation of "A Kiss to Build a Dream on." These choices of tracks were important to Fallout's world-building as each provides a connection to the retro futuristic aesthetic that the Fallout series is known for. While the game still used some ambient music, *Fallout: Brotherhood of Steel* diverged from this approach wildly during its boss battles, as its soundtrack featured songs from then-contemporary metal bands: "The Heretic Anthem" by Slipknot and "My Last Serenade" by Killswitch Engage are two good examples of such tracks. Lafleuriel (2018: 55) described this approach as "an attempt to reach out to younger console players," though I suggest here that regardless of the reasoning, that attempt was misguided simply because of the obvious mismatch in aesthetics.

In comparison to *Fallout Tactics*, and indeed all of the other Fallout spinoff games, *Fallout: Brotherhood of Steel* is the least canonical: unlike *Fallout Tactics*, which is considered at least semi-canonical, Lafleuriel (2018: 55) notes that events of the game have been explicitly described by Bethesda as not canonical, claiming that "when Bethesda took over the license, it completely erased all traces of *Fallout: Brotherhood of Steel*." In fact, *Fallout: Brotherhood of Steel* is not listed on Bethesda's page for Fallout games, while all of the other spinoff games are, suggesting that the company is not interested in supporting or even acknowledging the game's existence. The game also has little connection to the original creators of the Fallout world: while the game was developed and published by Interplay, the same company that released the first two games, the development team for the game did not feature any of the original developers of the first two games. The game also has a negative reputation with developers of the franchise in general: in fact, Lafleuriel (2018: 55) argues that the game was one of the "'bad decisions' often cited by the creators of the first two *Fallout* games as reasons they left the company." Similarly, Frank Zelensky, a *Fallout 3* developer who joined the development team because he was a fan of the franchise in general, said of *Fallout: Brotherhood of Steel*:

> I so wanted it to be good, because it had been so very long since a good Fallout game. Nowadays, I keep the disc around solely to focus all of my hatred and scorn into it. But I try not to actually touch it, lest its fundamental badness rub off on me.
>
> (Fallout Wiki)

Overall, I argue that *Fallout: Brotherhood of Steel* is an example of a world-building experiment that was not successful due to it not being faithful to elements of the Fallout world. That being said, its radical experimentation with such elements may have laid some groundwork for Fallout spinoff games to explore quite different approaches to the canon of Fallout like the one used in *Fallout Shelter*, which I discuss in the next section of this chapter.

Metacanonicity: Fallout Shelter

As noted in the previous sections, the much of the events of *Fallout Tactics* and *Fallout: Brotherhood of Steel* are both considered either semi-canonical or noncanonical, which might suggest that Fallout spinoffs are best suited to operating outside of the Fallout canon rather than attempting to create canonical expansions to the Fallout world. That logic also seems to inform Bethesda's mobile spinoff game, *Fallout Shelter*, which operates in an interesting liminal space in regard to Fallout canon. While I noted that the two spinoffs I discussed previously were not created by the original creators of the Fallout franchise, those games may have struggled to work within the Fallout canon because they were narrative-focused games: both *Fallout Tactics* and *Fallout: Brotherhood of Steel* tell specific stories within the

Fallout world, and many elements of those stories have been judged as inconsistent with the canon of that world. *Fallout Shelter*, on the other hand, does not have a narrative in the traditional sense: instead, the game has the player take on the role of a Vault Overseer managing a fictional vault within the Fallout universe. In essence, *Fallout Shelter* operates as an in-universe simulation of the Fallout world: rather than telling a canonical story about a specific part of the world, the game requires the player to construct their own noncanonical story about a fictional vault of their own design. I suggest that *Fallout Shelter* is an example of what I call *metacanonicty*, which I define as a form experimentation with a franchise's canon that operates both within and outside of its canonical bounds. It is also worth mentioning that there is a sequel to the game called *Fallout Shelter Online* (2019) that does have more narrative elements, but I have not included that game in this analysis because it is not currently available in Western markets and it is unclear if it will ever be released in those markets; at this time I am unable to access it.

A useful framework for looking at *Fallout Shelter*'s overall place in the world of Fallout might be considering how it fits into the world from a story perspective. The game could be described as an example of a noncanonical work created "by the world's own author or others authorized to produce them" (Wolf, 2012: 271), often in ways that are simply meant to expand the visibility of the world. Wolf (2012: 271) offers the example of Star Wars characters appearing in advertisements, which might seem similar to the situation of canonical Fallout characters showing up in *Fallout Shelter* vaults, a notion I discuss further below. Of course, the narratives of advertisements are not expected to fit into the canon of the world they take place in: Baby's Yoda's appearance in a commercial is obviously not part of *The Mandalorian's* (2019) story. As such, Wolf's (2012: 278) discussion of ancillary products might therefore also be useful here: he notes that such products "may not add to a world's canon, but they can change the way that a world and its assets are experienced." Considering that *Fallout Shelter* is clearly noncanonical and while also being the only Fallout game that is playable on mobile devices, it may simply be an example of an ancillary product designed to expand the player base for Fallout games. Lafleuriel (2018: 57) describes the game similarly as well, claiming that they game "helped to open up the saga to a more hard-to-reach audience" and framing it mostly as a kind of advertisement for *Fallout 4* since it was released on the same day as that game's trailer. These notions are useful in the sense that they describe Bethesda's likely intentions for making *Fallout Shelter* and how players often engage with the game, but they do not necessarily describe the actual in-universe narrative explanation for the game's story. Considering that story as noncanonical might therefore be too simple, and I suggest that metacanonicty is the most useful term for understanding what is going on with *Fallout Shelter* in terms of the game's in-world story: the game simply presents the player with an opportunity to create their own vault without offering a clear narrative explanation for who the player represents in the game world or whether the vault being created is a canonical one. Instead, players are left to construct their own explanation for how – or even if – the vault they create fits into the canonical world of Fallout.

I touched on the notion of *Fallout Shelter* operating as an ancillary product above, but it also worth noting that the game is the only "free to play" expansion of the Fallout world available. Such monetization models are especially common in mobile games, and such games usually rely on allowing the player to make small in-game purchases. Some of those purchases may be entirely cosmetic, offering no in-game advantage: for example, a character skin that allows a player to take on a different appearance in the game world. Others might be connected directly to gameplay, providing the player with more powerful items or faster access to special abilities. Such games are often described as "pay to win" games, a concept I have touched on in the past (Howard, 2019: 148): in essence, spending money in such games provides players with some kind of in-game benefit. I also noted in that article that such games operate on a spectrum in terms of how they approach such elements and that competitive games can especially encourage players to spend more (Howard, 2019: 151), but *Fallout Shelter* is different in that regard in that it has no multiplayer or competitive elements: it does not even have a clear win state as the player can simply continue working on a particular vault indefinitely. It might be described as a "pay to win" game in that most of its in-game purchases do offer direct advantages to players, but since there is no competitive advantage in doing so and all the purchasable content can be acquired through other means, it might be better described as a "pay to save time" game. From a canonicity perspective, the most interesting element of the game's approach to monetization is that unlike other games, which often offer some kind of "premium" currency that must be purchased and then spent on items in the game shop, *Fallout*

Shelter simply offers its in-game items for direct real-world prices. These purchases therefore seem to be metacanonical as well: there is no narrative explanation for where the items come from or why the "Mr. Handy" robot depicted in *Fallout Shelter*'s in-game shop accepts real-world currency.

As noted above, metacanonicty in *Fallout Shelter* is primarily exhibited in how the game functions in relationship to the canon of the Fallout world, but a final element of the game that is worth considering is the actual storyline presented within the game. When the game begins the player is tasked with choosing a three-digit number that represents the vault they will be managing: any number that fits within those parameters is an option, which means the player can choose a number corresponding to an existing vault within the Fallout canon. Doing so has no in-game effect, however: choosing a number corresponding to *Fallout 3*'s Vault 112, for example, is no different than choosing any other number, and the player is not required to adhere to the canonical version of what happened during the Vault 112 storyline in *Fallout 3*. Much of gameplay in *Fallout Shelter* centers around attracting various vault dwellers to inhabit the player's new vault, and while most of those characters are given generic names and appearances, from time to time a legendary vault dweller will appear: these characters represent specific named individuals from *Fallout 3* and *Fallout 4*. These legendary vault dwellers do not respect Fallout canon either and can appear in circumstances that clash wildly with their established stories: for example, Colonel Autumn is *Fallout 3*'s final antagonist, but he can also appear as a vault dweller and work amicably alongside James, the *Fallout 3* protagonisti's father, who attempts to kill Autumn during the events of *Fallout 3* and who dies in the process. Legendary vault dwellers are also not unique to a vault, such that several Colonel Autumns and Jameses can all operate independently within one vault. This scenario might appear to be reminiscent of the canonical clone-filled Vault 108 in *Fallout 3*, but unlike that vault, which contains cloning labs and holotapes explaining the situation, *Fallout Shelter* presents no clear narrative reason for why multiples of the same character can appear in one of the game's vaults: while players can build many structures inside their vaults in *Fallout Shelter*, a cloning lab is not among those options. Overall, events in *Fallout Shelter* clearly do not respect the canon of the Fallout franchise, though they do so in a referential way that is not necessarily intended to represent a canonical portrayal of the Fallout world. Freeman (2019: 25) also suggests a potential way of looking at this kind of situation using a historiographical approach that "[embraces] the plurality of fictional histories – acknowledging that, like history, an imaginary world is comprised of multiple, contradictory perspectives and reports that depend on context." In this sense, the events depicted in a particular *Fallout Shelter* vault might simply be considered one potential iteration of that vault's history rather than a history that is intended to be fully canonical and supporting the idea that those events are metacanonical. Such a view could be applied to most of the other Fallout spinoffs too, but the only spinoff game whose events are considered entirely canonical is *Fallout: New Vegas*, which I discuss in the next section of this chapter.

True Canonicity: *Fallout: New Vegas*

As mentioned above, *Fallout: New Vegas* has the distinction of being the only Fallout spinoff game that is considered fully canonical. Josh Sawyer (2012), the project lead on the game, noted that the development cycle of the game was relatively short, with the team only given 18 months to create the game. Because of that short development time much of *Fallout: New Vegas* is built with assets from *Fallout 3*, as the game uses the same engine and reuses things like character and item models, textures, sound effects, and much more. Similarly, the game uses some story elements of *Van Buren*, the cancelled version of *Fallout 3* that Interplay created in the early 2000s. The team that created the game also had some connections to the original *Fallout 1* and *Fallout 2* development teams: Obsidian Entertainment is a successor to Black Isle Studios, with many members of Black Isle going on to join Obsidian after Interplay closed. These factors lend an element of legitimacy to the game that may be one obvious reason for why it is often considered the only canonical Fallout spinoff game: the game relies on both design and narrative elements from all of the previous main Fallout games and even includes some of the franchise's original designers.

In terms of its story, *Fallout: New Vegas* takes place 40 years after the events of *Fallout 2* and returns to the western United States, essentially functioning as a sequel to the original two Fallout games. As such, *Fallout: New Vegas* offers some information about how the events of *Fallout 2* turned out. *Fallout: New Vegas* continues the critique of American colonialism that is found in *Fallout 1* and 2 by continuing the story of New California Republic, the democratic, expansionist state that rose from the small town of Shady Sands in *Fallout 1*. In *Fallout: New Vegas* the New California Republic has expanded even further: essentially all of the world map areas depicted in *Fallout 1* and *Fallout 2* are now under the control of the New California Republic, such that they control almost all of what was originally California and some of the surrounding areas. Most of the territory is no longer a lawless wasteland, as full-fledged cities with functioning governments and social systems exist in the New California Republic. Farming is the area's major industry, with many people herding Brahmin, the mutated two-headed cows that inhabit the Fallout world. While it is no utopia and the player does not get to directly see it and form their own opinions, by all accounts the New California Republic seems to be the most stable society in the Fallout world and its depiction seems to be a natural extension of its expansionist role in *Fallout 2*.

While it has some connections to the original developers of *Fallout 1* and *Fallout 2*, *Fallout: New Vegas*' canonicity may be tied to its alignment with many of the themes of previous Fallout games that critiqued American colonial expansionism and its focus on having the player taken an active role in that critique. The game continues the depiction of the New California Republic as a colonialist group: much of the game's plot centers on their encroachment into the Las Vegas area, a region known as the Mojave Wasteland, and the player's decision on whether to aid them or assist another group instead. The Mojave Wasteland is relatively dangerous when compared to the New California Republic's territory: Arjoranta (2017: 712) notes that when exploring the area "in addition to bandits and monsters, the player must be aware of the character's need for sustenance and of the harmful effects of radiation." The Mojave Wasteland centers around the city of New Vegas, a small city that mostly centers around the Las Vegas strip. The Strip, as it is known, is controlled by the enigmatic Mr. House, a man who no one has actually met, but who rules the area with an iron fist – almost literally, in fact, as his main method of enforcing his will is using his army of Securitron robots. Mr. House is not necessarily a tyrant, as much of The Strip's day-to-day politics are managed by various families who run the large casinos that fund the Strip's economy, but Mr. House also does not tolerate direct opposition, having driven out the previous inhabitants of the area, which include the descendants of The Khans. Mr. House and the New California Republic reached a truce before the events of the game began, but both are secretly working to assert control over the area during the game, and the game's main plot sees the player either going it alone, siding with one of them, or working with another major power in the area: Caesar's Legion, a slave-taking army of raiders who model themselves after the Roman Republic and who are also expanding into the area. The story of *Fallout: New Vegas* therefore centers around the colonial conflict over the Mojave Wasteland, a conflict primarily instigated by the expansion of the New California Republic and Caesar's Legion into the area. Much like the previous games, *Fallout: New Vegas* creates a politically charged context that will shape the future of the Fallout world, and the player must take an active role in that situation as part of the game's story.

Given the player's active role in *Fallout: New Vegas'* main story, it is worth briefly addressing here the element of role-playing inherent to the Fallout world. In *Fallout: New Vegas*, the player is playing as The Courier, a fictional character in a fictional world. Like many role-playing games, *Fallout: New Vegas* creates a connection between player and character that implies an active emotional role in the game's story. McMahon, Wyeth, and Johnson (2012: 116) discuss this connection in a study of 116 *Fallout: New Vegas* players that looked at the relationship between their Myers-Briggs personality types and play styles, suggesting that by looking at such relationships "we are able to develop assumptions about how personality influences the play styles that people bring to a game like [*Fallout: New Vegas*]." Similarly, Leino (2015: 170–174) highlights this relationship in the context of romancing one of the game's characters, calling it "love in bad faith" because it acknowledges the genuineness of the player's feelings for what they know is a fictional character. While my analysis focuses more on the world of Fallout and less on the player's relationship to it, I argue that *Fallout: New Vegas* does something similar with its political elements, especially since the game ends with a "slide show" that accounts for the player's actions by showing their impact on almost every part of the game world. This could perhaps be described as "world-building in bad faith," especially if the player sides with a group like Caesar's Legion: I can certainly attest to my own uncomfortable emotions when doing a "Legion playthrough" of the game and condemning the region to slavery. Of course, examining the player's impact on the world is a theme of the franchise as a whole, and almost all of the Fallout games do this to some extent

– notably, *Fallout 4* used a very similar approach, which I discussed in the previous chapter – but *Fallout: New Vegas* foregrounds it quite significantly, with the main story of the game centering almost entirely on the player's impact on the political landscape of the Fallout world. This connection to one of the core themes of the Fallout series may be why *Fallout: New Vegas* is considered canonical.

It is also worth noting that before *Fallout: New Vegas* began, several important events shaped the history and structure of the conflicts in the region and that are also an extension of the Fallout world's critique of American militarism, tying it to the themes of the other canonical Fallout games. The first battle of the Hoover Dam might be the most central of these events: it saw the New California Republic and Caesar's Legion clashing for control of the dam in one of the first true large-scale conflicts between the groups. The New California Republic was able to hold off Caesar's Legion, but the battle took a massive toll on the group, though it did allow them to secure most of the region. Another one of those events was the Bitter Springs Massacre, a conflict between the New California Republic and the Great Khans, a group descended from the Khans depicted in *Fallout 1*. The Great Khans were based out of Bitter Springs and were the last major threat to the New California Republic's control of the region after they drove out Caesar's Legion, and after intense raiding by The Great Khans the New California Republic decided to attack Bitter Springs. The intelligence they gathered indicated that the location was a raider stronghold, but that turned out to be incomplete: it also housed the group's women, children, elderly, and infirm. Both events are obvious critiques of militarism: the Battle of Hoover Dam sees two large armed forces clashing over the area's water supply in an attempt to control the region, while the Bitter Springs Massacre sees soldiers killing innocents. Such events are also well in line with the themes of previous Fallout games, with the Battle of Hoover Dam in particular recalling the battle over the water purifier at the Jefferson Memorial in *Fallout 3* and the Bitter Springs massacres depicting the continued marginalization of the Khans by the expansionist New California Republic.

The Great Khans storyline in *Fallout: New Vegas* also continues in the Fallout franchise's critique of American colonialism and expansionism by picking up on the Khans storyline from *Fallout 1* and *Fallout 2*. *Fallout 2* establishes that The Khans were almost completely eliminated by the main character of *Fallout 1*, allowing Shady Sands to expand and become the burgeoning New California Republic.

Similarly, *Fallout: New Vegas* establishes that the New Khans of *Fallout 2* were driven out by The Chosen One, allowing the New California Republic to annex their territory, but some survived to carry on the traditions of the group, establishing The Great Khans in the New Vegas region. The game depicts the group as living in Red Rock Canyon, having fled there after their defeat at Bitter Springs: they now survive in a harsh wilderness where they cannot grow crops to sustain themselves, resorting primarily to drug trafficking and raiding to support themselves. The Great Khans have not been depicted since their appearance in *Fallout: New Vegas*, so there is no canonical end to their story at the moment. That being said, it is worth noting that there is no ending to *Fallout: New Vegas* in which the group maintains a presence in the region: there are too many endings to summarize, but in general they either leave the area, fall apart, and lose their identity as a distinct group or are betrayed by the New California Republic after an alliance with them. While future entries in the series may portray a different outcome for the group, the consistent marginalization of The Khans by expansionist groups suggests that their role in the world of Fallout will always serve as a critique of such American colonialism.

Conclusion: The Many Shapes of the World of Fallout

In this chapter I have examined the various Fallout spinoff games through the lens of canonicity: these games mostly have a fraught relationship to the Fallout canon, with *Fallout: New Vegas* standing as the only spinoff game that is considered fully canonical. That being said, such games have shown that a logic of reinvention runs throughout the world of Fallout: it has taken many different shapes and gameplay styles, with the most effective incarnations staying true to the franchise's core themes. There are no Fallout spinoff games currently on the horizon, so it is difficult to predict if any future spinoffs will be considered canonical as well, though Bethesda's next main Fallout games, *Fallout 5*, is so far off that a spinoff might be possible. Rumors about a potential *Fallout: New Vegas* sequel spinoff game have certainly been popular, however, and those rumors intensified after Microsoft bought both ZeniMax, Bethesda's parent company, and Obsidian Entertainment, the developer that made *Fallout: New Vegas*. Numerous gaming journalism articles have since speculated about the situation: for example, Video Game Chronicle published an article claiming that the "original developer Obsidian could create a sequel to the classic RPG, now that it's under the same roof as license holder Bethesda" (Middler, 2022), and Gamebyte similarly published an article about rumors that the game might be coming (Hayton, 2021). That being said, in an interview with Feagus Urquhart, Obsidian Entertainment's CEO, Urquhart responded to a question about his ideas for a potential new Fallout game by saying "we're not working on *Fallout,* and we haven't even talked about what it would be" (Sosnowski, 2023). At the moment, then, there are no more Fallout spinoffs on the horizon, and it is possible that the series' issues with canonicity may be in the past.

In the next chapter I expand my analysis even further, looking to fan-created content for the Fallout world. As I noted in the introduction to this chapter, *Fallout 76* could be considered a spinoff game created by Bethesda, but the majority of the game's content is created by players, such that it fits well with the other fan creations that I examine in Chapter 4. Mods expand the world of Fallout even further, allowing players not only to create within the frameworks established by the game's developers but to expand the game into new territories that the base games did not originally support. Tabletop games allow players without modding skills to build their own parts of the Fallout world as well and also serve as a connection back to the franchise's origins in tabletop games. Overall, the logic of reinvention established by the Fallout spinoff games create an imaginary world to which video game developers, players, modders, and tabletop gamers can all contribute, and I turn my analysis to the fan-created components of the Fallout world in the next chapter.

References

Arjoranta, Jonne. 2017. 'Narrative Tools for Games: Focalization, Granularity, and the Mode of Narration in Games,' in *Games and Culture* 7–8, pp. 696–717.

Bethesda Game Studios, 2008. *Fallout 3.* Bethesda Softworks.

Bethesda Softworks. '*Fallout Tactics,*' *Bethesda.Net.* https://fallout.bethesda.net/en/games/fallout-tactics (accessed January 30, 2023).

Freeman, Matthew. 2019. *The World of the Walking Dead.* New York: Routledge.

Hayton, Phil. 2021. 'Rumor Claims *Fallout: New Vegas* 2 is Coming,' *Gamebyte* (January 19). https://www.gamebyte.com/fallout-new-vegas-2-is-coming-claims-rumour/ (accessed January 30, 2023).

Lafleuriel, Erwan. 2018. *Fallout: A Tale of Mutation: Creation – Universe – Decryption.* Toulouse: Third Editions.

Leino, Olli Tapio. 2015. ''I Know Your Type, You are a Player': Suspended fulfillment in *Fallout: New Vegas*,' in *Game Love: Essays on Play and Affection*, edited by Jessica Enevold and Esther McCallum-Stewart, pp. 165–178. Jefferson: McFarland.

Lessa, Rodrigo and Araújo, João. 2017. 'World Consistency,' in *The Routledge Companion to Imaginary Worlds*, edited by Mark J.P. Wolf, pp. 90–97. London: Routledge.

McCrea, Christian. 2013. 'Snapshot 4: Australian Video Games: The Collapse and Reconstruction of an Industry,' in *Gaming Globally: Production, Play, and Place (Critical Media Studies)*, edited by Nina B. Huntermann and Ben Aslinger, pp. 203–206. New York: Palgrave-McMillian.

McMahon, Nicole, Wyeth, Peta and Johnson, Daniel. 2012. 'Personality and Player Types in *Fallout: New Vegas*,' in *Proceedings of the 4th International Conference on Fun and Games*, pp. 113–116.

"Meet the *Fallout 3* Devs," *Fallout Wiki*, https://fallout.fandom.com/wiki/Fred_Zeleny/Meet_the_Fallout_3_devs (accessed January 30, 2023)

Middler, Jordan. 2022. 'Fallout New Vegas 2 is Reportedly in 'Very Early Talks at Microsoft',' *Video Games Chronicle* (February 24), https://www.videogameschronicle.com/news/fallout- new-vegas-2-is-reportedly-in-very-early-talks-at-microsoft/ (Accessed January 30, 2023).

Nguyen, Thierry. 2007. '*Fallout 3*,' *Gamespy* (July 1), http://pc.gamespy.com/pc/fallout-3/800771p1.html (accessed January 30, 2023).

Obsidian Entertainment. 2010. *Fallout: New Vegas.* Bethesda Softworks.

Proctor William and Freeman, Matthew. 2017. "The First Step Into a Smaller World': The Transmedia Economy of *Star Wars*,' in *Revisiting Imaginary Worlds: A Subcreation Studies Anthology*, edited by Mark J.P. Wolf, pp. 221–243. London: Routledge.

Sawyer, Josh. 2012. 'Do (Say) The Right Thing: Choice Architecture, Player Expression, and Narrative Design in *Fallout: New Vegas*,' *GDC Vault*, https://www.gdcvault.com/play/1015758/Do-(Say)-The-Right-Thing (accessed 30 January 2023).

Schulzke, Marcus. 2009. 'Moral Decision Making in Fallout,' in *Game Studies* 9(2).

Sosonowski, Hubert. 2023. "My Greatest Triumph? Obsidian Survived.' Interview with Feargus Urquhart,' *Gamepressure* (January 18), https://www.gamepressure.com/editorials/my- greatest-triumph-obsidian-survived-feargus-urquhart-interview/za604 (accessed January 30, 2023).

Walker, Mark H. 2000. 'Previews – Fallout: Tactics,' *CNET Gamecenter.com* (September 22). https://web.archive.org/web/20001212101100/ http://www.gamecenter.com/Pc/Previews/Fallout (accessed January 30, 2023).

Wolf, Mark J.P. 2012. *Building Imaginary Worlds: The Theory and History of Subcreation.* London: Routledge.

4 The World of Fallout as Told by Fans

Fallout 76, Fallout Mods, and *Fallout* Tabletop Games

In previous chapters of this book I have examined the world of Fallout as told by video game developers: the franchise has been worked on by many creators over the years, and as noted in the previous chapter, some of those creations have not been successful in terms of staying faithful to the canon of the Fallout series. That being said, those creations also established a logic of reinvention for the world of Fallout: it is a series that has been taken many forms and has therefore invited participation from a variety of people beyond its original creators, including its own fans. This kind of situation is not uncommon, as Duncan (2013: 85) points out, claiming that "as with many media, the lines between producer and consumer have become blurred" with regard to video games. In this chapter I extend my analysis of the world of Fallout to those fan creations, which are quite numerous and blur the lines between those making the Fallout games and those playing them. I also therefore approach the world of Fallout from a slightly different angle in this chapter that is worth mentioning: in previous chapters of this book, I looked at the world of Fallout as an "interactive world" (Wolf, 2012: 138): the kind of world that "changed the audience member's role from observer to participant" by allowing the player to make choices and impact the game world. In this chapter I look at Fallout through the framework of "participatory worlds" (Wolf, 2012: 281), which are slightly different: while Wolf highlights the fact that interactive worlds have participatory elements, he notes a key difference between the two: "participatory worlds are a subset of interactive worlds, since while all participatory worlds are inherently open and interactive, not all interactive worlds allow the user to make permanent changes to the world, sharing in its authorship." As such, in previous chapters I focused on single-player Fallout games that have interactive worlds, but not necessarily participatory ones: as

DOI: 10.4324/9781003395744-5

Wolf (2012: 281) notes, "single player video games, for example, allow interaction, but nothing the player does will result in a permanent change in the world's canon." Single-player video games do not encompass the entire experience of the Fallout world, however, and while there are participatory elements to Fallout's single-player games that I will briefly touch on in this chapter, my main focus is moving beyond the single-player experience in this chapter.

In this chapter I first look at fan creation in *Fallout 76* (2018), the most recent Fallout video game and the first to rely entirely on online multiplayer gameplay, as much of the game is centered around player-created content. I then examine gameplay modifications, more commonly referred to as mods, as modding the Fallout games is quite common and is a practice that has been with the franchise throughout its history. Finally, I analyze the various incarnations of Fallout tabletop games, which are a particularly interesting example of remediation given the Fallout world's roots in tabletop roleplay games that I touched on in Chapter 1. Overall, I argue that these practices allow players to engage in their own extensions of the Fallout world, expanding the franchise beyond the limits of the games themselves and offering fans a way to put their own mark on the world of Fallout.

Player-Driven World-Building: Fan Creation in *Fallout 76*

For most of its 25-year history the Fallout franchise was almost entirely a single-player experience: *Fallout Tactics* (2001) and *Fallout: Brotherhood of Steel* (2004) have multiplayer modes, but they were not the main focus and mostly functioned as a bonus on top of the single-player gameplay. The most recent game in the franchise, *Fallout 76*, changed that significantly, however: the game is played entirely online, and while it is possible to experience a fair amount of the game's content alone, the game is intended as a multiplayer experience. This can be seen by looking at the game's structure: there are many in-game events that cannot be completed without a team of players working together. At the game's release there were no non-player characters in the game to interact with either: all interpersonal interaction in the game at that point took place between players. Some of these design elements are tied to the timeline of *Fallout 76*: the game is set only 25 years after the world was destroyed in a nuclear apocalypse, and players of the game are depicted as being some of the first people to explore the wasteland after the bombs fell. The situation is quite similar to Freeman's (2019: 1) description of *The Walking Dead* franchise in another *Imaginary Worlds* series book: like the characters in that world, players in the world of *Fallout 76* "must work together not only to survive but to create a new world order with new social structures, new values, new modes of communication, and entirely new ways of living." Of course, in the case of *Fallout 76*, those characters are portrayed by players in an interactive environment, adding a participatory element to that depiction. Such changes might represent one of the most significant reinventions of the Fallout world thus far: before *Fallout 76*, most of the previous games were single-player narrative-driven role-playing games, so *Fallout 76* did not simply change small elements of the world but instead took an almost entirely different approach to the franchise by making a multiplayer game in which players themselves create the narrative.

It is worth noting that *Fallout 76* was not particularly successful in terms of critical and fan reactions when it was launched, making it the only Fallout game aside from *Fallout: Brotherhood of Steel* (2004) to hold that dubious honor. Examining reviews from video game journalism websites around the time of its release reveals some common themes in these negative reactions, many of which center around the game moving away from the single-player narrative-driven experience that the Fallout franchise was known for. A *Gamespot* review provides a good example of this kind of criticism, arguing that *Fallout 76*

> introduces significant changes to the set structure of *Fallout 4* to make it function as both a single-player and multiplayer experience. In doing so, both styles of play suffer from major compromises that exist only to serve the other, and as a result, both are weak.
>
> (Tran, 2018)

Many reviews highlighted this move away from a more focused single-player experience as one of the game's most significant issues, and some even commented on the lackluster multiplayer experience: a *PC Gamer* review noted that "it's a relief so much of *Fallout 76* can be tackled alone, and in some cases it's actually better that way" (Livingston, 2018). The game has received numerous updates since its release, however, and those do seem to have improved the situation, with *GameRant* claiming that "several improvements, in particular, have made *Fallout 76* an RPG worth playing in 2022" (Anaya, 2022). That being said, it is difficult to ignore the game's rocky reception considering the successes of most other Fallout games, and much of that reception seems to be tied to the game attempting to function effectively as both a single-player and multiplayer experience and not succeeding at either.

Much of *Fallout 76*'s gameplay is drawn from the previous game in the series, *Fallout 4* (2015): in particular, crafting and base building are core elements of the experience, perhaps even more so than in the previous game. As in *Fallout 4*, in *Fallout 76* the player can construct settlements with buildings, defensive turrets, storage containers, and much more using the game's Construction and Assembly Mobile Platform system, with these settlements being referred to as C.A.M.P.s. While *Fallout 4* offered specific locations where settlements could be built, *Fallout 76* expands that system to almost the entire game world: players can build C.A.M.P.s nearly anywhere, with the only restrictions being that those C.A.M.P.s cannot be built too close to other existing locations or other player created settlements. Players can also collaborate on C.A.M.P.s together, though each one is assigned to a particular player and cannot be edited or interacted with if that player is no longer online. Building a particular structure or item in a C.A.M.P.s requires item blueprints that can be found throughout the game world, but players also have another option for building settlements: using one of the game's many Public Workshops. These allow players to craft things that they do not have the blueprints for, though they come with a downside, as such settlements are publicly available to all players on a given server and players can attempt to attack and take control of Public Workshops from other players.

While the C.A.M.P. system is one of *Fallout 76*'s biggest changes to the overall Fallout gameplay structure, it does represent perhaps one of the most direct avenues for player-generated content in the entire series. As noted in the previous chapter, *Fallout 4* allows the player to build settlements, but that system is optional: in fact, it is entirely possible to almost completely ignore the settlement system in *Fallout 4* other than completing a brief required tutorial near the beginning of the game. On the other hand, *Fallout 76* makes the C.A.M.P. system a core component of gameplay: creating a home base to stash your belongings, repair your equipment, and craft items is essentially required, with the game being designed around the idea that the player will venture out into the wasteland, gather materials, and return to their home base to build it up further. In fact, a 2021 game update enabled a

C.A.M.P slot system, allowing the player to build multiple C.A.M.P.s, though only one can be active at any given time. As such, player-created content is a central component of *Fallout 76*, and a player is likely to encounter quite a bit of content created by other players while playing. Of course, players can only create content that was explicitly enabled by the game's developers, so there are still some limitations on the kinds of content that players can create in *Fallout 76*. Traditionally, those limitations could be bypassed using mods, though because *Fallout 76* is an online game, mods are not officially supported and there are no modding tools available for the game. Mods do exist for the game, but they do not make the kinds of dramatic visual and gameplay changes that mods for previous Fallout games do; as such, I turn to looking at mods for some of the previous Fallout games in the next section.

Visual Enhancements, Gameplay Changes, and Total Conversions: Modding the World of Fallout

While *Fallout 76* was the first Fallout game to truly rely on player-created content for the majority of its world-building, Fallout players were getting involved in world-building long before that game was released, primarily through creating modifications for the Fallout games. Making mods and modding (the terms I will use throughout this book) is a common practice for video games, so much so that some companies release official modding tools for their own games. Mods have been popular throughout the history of the Fallout franchise, and especially since Bethesda took ownership of the series, as the company has a long history of supporting mods for their games in various ways. This section will first look at mods for Bethesda's Fallout games because mods for their games are the most numerous and often make very dramatic and noticeable visual changes to the games, an approach used in many mods for all of Bethesda's games. I will then look at three specific mods, two for *Fallout 2* (1998) and one for *Fallout: New Vegas* (2010), that make significant gameplay changes to their respective games; I suggest that these mods have a connection to Fallout's tabletop gaming roots, bearing many similarities to how tabletop gamers expand and reinvent the rules of the games they play. Finally, I look at Fallout total conversion mods, a special category of mod that essentially serves as an entirely standalone experience separate from the game it was originally based on. Overall, I argue that mods allow fans to participate in world-building for the Fallout franchise in a similar fashion to how fans participate in world-building in *Fallout 76* and Fallout tabletop games.

It is worth addressing an issue related to modding before looking at some specific examples of Fallout mods: the problem of companies relying on modders to fix elements of their game worlds. While *Fallout 1* (1997) and *Fallout 2* did not have modding tools available and were released in the late 1990s when post-release patches and bug fixes were not especially common, both games did receive some support after they were released, though patches for the games were not able to address all of the bugs they had. Most of the later Fallout games, on the other hand, had mod support and were released in an era where post-release patching was considered common. That being said, those games still had unfixed bugs after they stopped receiving official developer support: this is not necessarily too surprising considering the scope of modern video games, as fixing every issue in modern video games is not always feasible. Mod support offers developers another avenue for addressing such issues, however, as they can simply allow fans to fix problems with games that the developers could not solve. Relying on community labor for bug fixing is certainly questionable, however, and Consalvo (2013: 127–128) notes that "the unpaid nature of this labor creates a particular stress" that often leads to many fandriven projects falling apart. This approach becomes even more problematic when it comes to issues like bad representation in games, as it often puts the work of addressing those kinds of topics on the very people who are being marginalized. While I have discussed this issue more in depth in both an article (2019: 9) and my dissertation (2021: 77), it is worth pointing out here as well simply because it is a problem that should not be ignored: in fact, several of the mods I discuss below are specifically aimed at fixing bugs in their base games and expanding the kinds of representation that those games support, such that they provide clear examples of the fan community putting in extra labor above and beyond what the original developers of the games were willing to do to address problems in their favorite game worlds.

When considering video game mods, it is important to note that video game mods are not all alike: they can fall into many different categories in terms of how they modify gameplay. Welch (2018) broadly classified mods into two categories: cosmetic enhancements, "or the swapping and appropriation of assets in the game in order to evoke or augment the player's relationship to that game," and mechanical alterations, which "change the rules and systems of gameplay to allow for emergent gameplay possibilities." Though Welch was specifically discussing queer video game mods in this context, such a division makes sense for many kinds of video game mods and is in line with other scholarship on modding: for example, Pereira and Bernardes (2022: 4) describe the various kinds of video game mods in a similar fashion, noting that "there are mods focused on upgrading a game's graphics, others on fixing bugs or restoring lost and cut features, and still others on enhancing mechanics and user interface or adding new content." Pereira and Bernardes (2022: 4) also highlight total conversion mods, many of which "completely [overhaul] the original base-game;" there are several Fallout mods that fall into this category, one of which I will discuss later in this section. These frameworks also apply well to mods for the Fallout series, many of which achieve similar goals; while I will not attempt to create a similar classification system for all the different kinds of Fallout mods in this section, I will examine some Fallout mods using the framework of cosmetic enhancements, mechanical alterations, and total conversion mods, as they represent some of the most common ways that Fallout fans use modding to expand the franchise's world.

As noted earlier, mods for Bethesda's single-player Fallout games, *Fallout 3* (2008) and *Fallout 4*, are especially popular because the company has a long history of offering modding support for their games. Modding tools for Bethesda's games have also remained fairly consistent over time, allowing fans to bring their modding experience from other Bethesda games, such as The Elder Scrolls series, to the Fallout franchise. The modding tools for the Fallout games are called the Garden of Eden Creation Kit, referencing the in-universe item that allows characters to create new communities from scratch. The tools are not perfect, as Hamalainen, Alnajjar, and Poibeau (2022) note when using the tools to extract dialogue from *Fallout: New Vegas* for a study: "the problem we ran into was that GECK is rather buggy." That being said, Bethesda's modding tools allow players to make significant alterations to their games, and some of the most popular mods for Bethesda games are the kinds of cosmetic enhancements described by Welch. Without surveying modders themselves it would be difficult to determine why that is the case, but a simple explanation might be that many kinds of cosmetic enhancements do not necessarily require any programming: swapping assets in the manner that Welch described can often be accomplished without writing any code. Of course, the kind of visual changes seen in a more complex cosmetic enhancement mod like torcher's (2017) "*Fallout 4* Texture Optimization Project" require going beyond the official mod tools offered by Bethesda, but adding a new weapon model like Cumble's (2018) "Riot Shotgun (*Fallout 4* Edition)" can be done relatively easily. That being said, such mods often make significant visual alterations to the game: for example, bxbblegumbxtch's (2016) "Boibomb – A Femboy CBBE Preset" offers "femboy" character models for *Fallout 4* that certainly stand out in comparison to the aesthetic of standard characters in the base game. While such mods rarely make mechanical changes to the games, cosmetic enhancements such as these are typically aimed at making aesthetic changes to the world and in many cases are quite effective at expanding a game's mood, tone, and feel in ways that were not supported in the base game. As such, the potential for cosmetic enhancements to expand a game world should not be underestimated, and they often offer ways for people who are not represented within a particular world to create their own personal connection to it.

While cosmetic enhancements for the Fallout games are mostly a phenomenon related to the Bethesda Fallout games because those games offer modding tools that make it easy to add new visuals to the games, mechanical alterations for their games also exist. These often take the form of "balance" mods that change values within the game in attempt to address potentially overpowered weapons or skills, mods that add entirely new mechanics to the game, or even mods that bring in mechanics from other games. Gameplay mods for Bethesda's games might be slightly less numerous than cosmetic mods because they are more likely to require some kind of programming and going beyond the official modding tools, but mechanical alterations also predate those games, which might be surprising since those games do not have any kind of modding support. Mods that alter gameplay mechanics also occupy an interesting space in relationship to the Fallout world specifically, however, because of Fallout's own connection to tabletop gaming. Tabletop gaming has a long history of experimentation with game mechanics and rules: nearly every version of Dungeons & Dragons (D&D) suggests players can and should change any element of the game system they do not like, while Generic Universal Roleplaying System (GURPS) encourages players to experiment with the basics of the world itself by choosing their own setting. Three mechanical alterations for the Fallout series are therefore particularly interesting given their specific goals: the *Fallout 2* unofficial patch and *Fallout 2* restoration project mods created by Killapp and the JSawyer mod for *Fallout: New Vegas* created by Josh Sawyer. All three of these mods have very similar aims in that they address bugs, balance issues, and cut contents for their respective games: they are not only gameplay mods but mods that attempt to provide the "true" experience for their respective game worlds.

As mentioned earlier, some mods focus on fixing problems with the original game, and Killapp's *Fallout 2* unofficial patch mod is a good example of such a mod aimed directly at bug fixing. *Fallout 2* received a few patches after its release in 1998, but the final official patch left numerous bugs unaddressed. Killapp's *Fallout 2* unofficial patch attempted to address these bugs, though the mod went through many releases over the years, with the most recent "official" update on Killapp's own website coming on July 5th, 2014. Killapp's *Fallout 2* restoration project mod is compatible with the unofficial patch, with both being designed to function together. The restoration project mod is aimed at restoring cut content to *Fallout 2*: a fair chunk of the game had to be removed before it was released due to time con-straints, though information about that content is still in the game files and some of the developers have spoken publicly about what some of the content was. The restoration project adds much of this content back to the game, some of which is quite significant: for example, the mod restores an entire dungeon, the Environmental Protection Agency, back to the game, along with numerous quests, characters, dialogue choices, and other content related to the area. Like the unofficial patch, the restoration project was built progressively over time, with the final "official" update posted simultaneously with the final unofficial patch update in 2014. The mods are especially impressive given the lack of modding tools for the first two Fallout games, as Killapp had figure out how to handle the bug fixes and restore the cut content without the kinds of tools available to those who make mods for Bethesda's later games. The situation resembles the kind of "ROM hacking" that fans of Japanese games that have not been released in America had to do, in which modders "reverse engineer the game code and work with-out documentation or support from the developer" (Consalvo, 2013: 123–124). As such, Killapp's mods represent significant fan-created expansions of the Fallout world, ones made even more impressive due to the effort required to create them without official modding tools.

As noted in the previous chapter, *Fallout: New Vegas* served as a sequel to the first two games in many ways, returning to the same region and following up on storylines and events from those games. Unlike *Fallout 2*, however, *Fallout: New Vegas* also had full modding support as it offered the same kinds of modding tools that *Fallout 3* did, making mods much easier to create. *Fallout: New Vegas* received many official patches after release, though various unofficial fan patch mods exist to fix bugs that were not fixed by the final official patch in a similar fashion to Killapp's. Perhaps the most interesting of these is the "JSawyer" mod created by Josh Sawyer, the game's lead designer and director. The JSawyer mod is different from these other mods in that it has more of an "official" aura, however: it is not an official patch for the game, but it was created by someone who actually worked on the game, implying that the gameplay changes and fixes it made represent the developer's vision for how its gameplay should work. The mod is much smaller in scale than Killapp's mods and does not focus too heavily on restoring cut content, instead fixing the implementation of some mechanics to reflect their intended design and making some balance changes that bring the game's mechanics more in line with the mechanics of the first two games. Of course, Josh Sawyer had some clear advantages in creating this mod: not only did modding tools exist for *Fallout: New Vegas*, he actually worked on the game himself and could make more extensive changes to the game given direct access to the game assets, which modding tools do not always allow for.

Much like Killapp, Josh Sawyer no longer maintains the JSawyer mod, which is unsurprising given that he actively works within the gaming industry: at the time of this writing he still works for Obsidian and was recently the project leader on *Pentiment* (2022). All the mods described above, however, have lived on and are continually updated by fans: Killapp's mods are maintained on public GitHub repositories, a website that allows users to post and share code projects, including games, and received updates as recently as December 2022. Similarly, an updated version of the JSawyer mod is available on NexusMods, one of the most popular modding websites, and was also updated in December 2022. While the current versions of these mods are no longer connected to their original creators, this process is relatively common in the modding community: Morshirnia and Walker (2007: 6) call it reciprocal innovation, a practice in which "a user may create the code for a modification, share her code for her modification, which may inspire another user to adopt/adapt the modification, which will in turn inspire further modification." All of the current versions of these mods could be seen as part of this phenomenon, and the fact that all of them have now become a part of the larger fan community shows the desire of the Fallout fanbase to not only expand its world but even expand on fan creations for that world.

While the mods described above are fairly extensive in terms of reinventing the Fallout world, one category of mods, called total conversion mods, goes even a step further. Total conversion mods are not limited to the Fallout series and can reimagine games in quite radical ways: for example, Robert Yang's (2015) *Radiator 1*, a total conversion mod for Valve's popular first-person shooter *Half-Life 2* (2004), creates a totally new experience about "stargazing, gay divorce, and Emily Dickinson." Fallout total conversion mods typically take a different approach, often focusing on a part of the story that has been unexplored in any parts of the official games. This is the case for *Fallout: New California* (Radiant-Helix Media, 2020), a fan-made total conversion mod that is a prequel to *Fallout: New Vegas*. The player character of *Fallout: New Vegas* has a deliberately nebulous background: the main game simply portrays the character as a courier working in the wasteland, while the "Lonesome Road" expansion provides a backstory in which the character was somehow responsible for the destruction of a town called Hopeville, though how exactly that happened is not fully explained. *Fallout: New California* connects some of these dots in a prequel story that sees the player escaping from a destroyed Vault and then becoming involved in a conflict between the New California Republic and an alliance of raiders, which includes their long-time nemesis The Khans. The mod is quite extensive, allowing the player to side with many different potential groups, including the villainous Enclave, though the mod's story always ends with the player losing touch with their allies, accidentally destroying Hopeville, and deciding to start over as a courier, tying up some of the loose ends of *Fallout: New Vegas*'s story. Interestingly, total conversion mods also have a connection to tabletop gaming: tabletop games often similarly require creating entirely new experiences within an existing framework, such as creating a series of adventures within a particular D&D world. While the Fallout world has many connections to tabletop games like GURPS and Gamma World that I touched on in Chapter 1, it also has a more direction connection to tabletop gaming: the *Fallout Tabletop Roleplaying Game* (2021). I look more directly at that game, as well as at the other Fallout tabletop games, in the next section of this chapter.

From Tabletop to PC and Back Again: The World of Fallout in Tabletop Games

As noted in Chapter 1 of this book, the world of Fallout has its roots in tabletop games: in particular, *Fallout 1* was originally built using the GURPS tabletop role-playing game rules set and was only switched over to Fallout's iconic S.P.E.C.I.A.L. system quite late in development. That connection has waxed and waned over the years, with the first two games having especially strong mechanical connections to tabletop gaming, and even the first spinoff, *Fallout Tactics*, not straying too far from those roots. Later games lost their direct mechanical connection to turn-based tabletop role-playing games when Fallout became a real-time action role-playing game franchise, but gameplay elements like the S.P.E.C.I.A.L. system have remained a mainstay of the series. That being said, the world of Fallout has made its own forays into tabletop gaming, as there have been numerous versions of Fallout tabletop games over the years. In this section I will look at those games more broadly before focusing specifically on the *Fallout: The Tabletop Roleplaying Game* (2021). I suggest all of these games provide an interesting example of what Bolter and Grusin call remediation because of the additional layer involved: they are tabletop game remediations of a video game series that itself originated as a remediation of a tabletop role-playing game rules system.

Before looking at the *Fallout: The Tabletop Roleplaying Game*, it is worth noting that a few other Fallout board games also exist, as well as a set of rules for tabletop gameplay provided alongside one of the video games. This section will look more in-depth at the tabletop role-playing game simply because of the Fallout world's overall strong connection to tabletop role-playing games, but the other games are worth briefly mentioning as they also represent significant iterations of the franchise in physical media. Fallout: Warfare was one of the first forays into tabletop gaming within the Fallout franchise, though it was not actually a standalone product: instead, rules for the game and imagery were provided on a bonus disc for *Fallout Tactics* (2001), the first Fallout spinoff game. The game strongly resembles Warhammer tabletop games: players create armies using the game rules and printed paper tokens that represent those armies and then do battle with one another on a tabletop, though there is no particular storyline or narrative arc for those battles and games can last as long as necessary to resolve the battle. *Fallout: The Board Game*

(2017) takes a more traditional approach to board gaming in that it is designed for single-session experiences lasting a few hours at most rather than long form multi-session tabletop campaigns. It also focuses on specific storylines drawn from *Fallout 3* and *Fallout 4* rather than encouraging players to create their own stories, with two expansion packs, the "New California" expansion and the "Atomic Bonds Upgrade" expansion, that include additional scenarios that are mostly drawn from those games. *Fallout Shelter: The Board Game* (2020) takes a similar approach in that it is also designed to be a single-session experience lasting only a couple of hours, though it is essentially a recreation of the video game in board game form and therefore does not have a significant narrative other than managing a vault. These board games are all interesting in that they provide different examples of how a video game might be recreated as a board game, though they are less interesting in terms of expanding the Fallout world: while they do adapt that world into a new medium, they do not expand the world itself since they are based on existing stories from the games or do not actually have a story.

Unlike the other games mentioned above, *Fallout: The Tabletop Roleplaying Game* functions as a full-on recreation of the Fallout world, working much like similar tabletop role-playing games like D&D: it provides the rules and contents necessary to create long-form multi-session gaming experiences with stories that can last for weeks, months, or even years. Much like other tabletop role-playing games, the game relies on a game master who manages gameplay and creates conflicts for the players to overcome along with accompanying narrative elements while each other player takes control of a particular character in the game world and dictates what that character does in response to in-game events. The game is based on the 2d20 system, a gaming system created by Modiphius Entertainment, a company that has created a number of licensed tabletop games based on various popular franchises. This means that the tabletop game does not attempt to reconstruct Fallout's mechanics, though many iconic elements of the Fallout world, such as the S.P.E.C.I.A.L. system, are still in place. Instead, the game's goal is to provide a playable tabletop role-playing game experience that is faithful to the aesthetics of the Fallout world without getting bogged down in fully recreating its mechanics, a task that might be difficult considering that the video games rely on computer code to handle the complicated math that goes into things like the game's firearms.

Fallout: The Tabletop Roleplaying Game is structured much like other tabletop role-playing games in that its core content is contained in lengthy, detailed rulebooks that outline how the game works and that are intended to provide players with a framework for creating their own content for the game world. Baker (2017: 83) argues that such books "foreground the process of creating secondary world elements, including characters, locations, material, and magic," all of which is true about *Fallout: The Tabletop Roleplaying Game* as well, with science fiction elements such as mutations taking the place of magic. At the time of this writing, there is a starter set aimed at providing a more streamlined introduction to the game that comes with pre-generated characters and a book with various quests that the characters can complete as well as a much lengthier core rulebook providing everything one needs to create content and run adventures in the system. There is also a quest book available that comes with the starter set that does contain potential stories for the players to work with, though like most tabletop role-playing games, the game master usually handles the overarching narrative of the game: the game master might use the pre-existing stories in the quest book directly, incorporate some elements of those stories into their own story, or simply create their own entirely original story. This structure mirrors other popular fantasy tabletop role-playing games like D&D, as Baker (2017: 84) suggests that material for such games typically falls into two categories: what he refers to as "organizational world infrastructures (timelines, etc., packaged for ready-made campaign settings)" and what he calls "generative world-building material — subcreation tools accompanied by DIY guidance in rulebooks and other products." Given the Fallout world's strong connection to tabletop role-playing games, it is unsurprising that its own tabletop role-playing game is organized in such a similar way.

An interesting element of all these games is how they remediate the Fallout video games into a tabletop format. Remediation, a term first coined by Bolter and Grusin (1999: 4–5), is described as a "contradictory... double logic" in which media both look back to older forms of media while also trying to replace them. Bolter (2001: 23) further discusses the notion while touching on the evolution of writing media, arguing that "we might call each such shift a 'remediation' in the sense that a new medium takes the place of an older one, borrowing and reorganizing the characteristics of writing in the older medium and reforming its cultural space." A similar situation occurred with tabletop role-playing-based video games, which remediated their analog counterparts in a digital setting: as I noted in Chapter 1, many of *Fallout 1*'s role-playing game contemporaries were based on the D&D franchise, and these games often reinvented elements of the tabletop games on which they were based to make them work in a digital setting. In the case of the Fallout franchise and its tabletop games, an additional element is present, however: the Fallout tabletop games are remediating a video game series that was originally based on a tabletop gaming ruleset in the first place. As noted in Chapter 1, the Fallout series was originally based on the GURPS, a very popular tabletop role-playing game system. While licensing issues prevented the final version of *Fallout 1* from actually using the GURPS, many elements of that system influenced the design of Fallout's S.P.E.C.I.A.L. system and the games have therefore always had a strong connection to tabletop role-playing games. As such, the Fallout tabletop games not only represent remediations of the video games into a physical format but also function almost like a return to the franchise's tabletop roots: they also demonstrate that while in its original conception remediation operates on a double logic, remediation in the Fallout franchise operates on a triple logic. I argue that this phenomenon is not limited to the Fallout world – in fact, I suggest that many imaginary worlds illustrate that remediation can move far beyond a double logic, especially those that have transmedia elements – and in the next chapter I look toward Fallout's forays into other forms of media beyond games.

Conclusion: How Fans Expanded the World of Fallout

This chapter has examined the world of Fallout through the lens of participatory worlds and fan creation, as Fallout is a series that offers numerous avenues for fans to participate in the construction of its universe. Mods for Fallout have existed through the franchise's history, giving fans with the necessary technical skills to get involved in creating content for the video games. Tabletop versions of Fallout, especially *The Fallout Tabletop Roleplaying Game*, allow those with world-building skills to create Fallout content without even needing the technical skills required to make a mod. *Fallout 76* draws on all of these various fan-driven traditions, creating a game in which the majority of the content itself is created by players. Wolf's discussion of participatory worlds might therefore be the best way to understand

The World of Fallout as Told by Fans 93

how the world of Fallout functions, though these fan creations are not necessarily canonical in the way that some fan-created participatory content is. That being said, as I discussed in the previous chapter, canon is already a fraught concept when discussing Fallout, and player-created content being noncanonical might make it no less legitimate than the content found in some actual Fallout spinoff games.

While I have looked at almost everything related to the Fallout world in previous chapters, I have still mostly kept my focus to Fallout games: almost everything Fallout-related so far has had some kind of ludic element. I have also generally avoided commenting directly on successes or failures in the franchise, with my discussion of canonicity in Chapter 3 perhaps being the closest I have gone toward that kind of analysis. The Fallout world has seen many successes and failures of world-building over the years, however, and offers many useful examples to world-builders of what success and failure might look like. In addition, Fallout's references to and expansions into non-game media offer some lessons for designers, especially those interested in transmedia storytelling. In the concluding chapter I turn to those concepts, looking beyond fan-created media into the wider world of Fallout.

References

Anaya, Christopher Julian. 2022. 'Is *Fallout 76* Worth Playing in 2022?,' *Gamerant* (July 22), https://gamerant.com/fallout-76-worth-playing-buying-2022/ (accessed January 30, 2023).

Baker, Neal. 2017. 'Secondary World Infrastructures and Tabletop Fantasy Role-playing Games,' in *Revisiting Imaginary Worlds: A Subcreation Studies Anthology*, edited by Mark J.P. Wolf, pp. 83–95. London: Routledge.

Bolter, Jay David. 2001. *Writing Spaces: Computers, Hypertext, and the Remediation of Print*, 2nd edition. New York: Routledge.

Bolter, Jay David and Grusin, Richard. 1999. *Remediation: Understanding New Media*. Cambridge: The MIT Press.

bxbblegumbxtch. 2016. 'Boibomb – A Femboy CBBE Bodyslide Preset,' *Nexusmods* (December 26), https://www.nexusmods.com/fallout4/mods/20836 (accessed January 30, 2023).

Consalvo, Mia. 2013. 'Unintended Travel: ROM Hackers and Fan Translations of Japanese Video Games,' in *Gaming Globally: Production, Play, and Place (Critical Media Studies)*, edited by Nina B. Huntermann and Ben Aslinger, pp 119–139. New York: Palgrave-McMillian.

Cumble. 2018. 'Riot Shotgun (*Fallout 4* Edition),' *Nexusmods* (April 28), https://www.nexusmods.com/fallout4/mods/30087 (accessed January 30, 2023).

Duncan, Sean C. 2013. 'Snapshot 3: Crafting a Path into Gaming Culture,' in *Gaming Globally: Production, Play, and Place (Critical Media Studies),* edited by Nina B. Huntermann and Ben Aslinger, pp. 85–89. New York: Palgrave-McMillian.

Freeman, Matthew. 2019. *The World of the Walking Dead.* New York: Routledge.

Hämäläinen, Mika, Alnajjar, Khalid and Poibeau, Theirry. 2022. 'Video Games as a Corpus: Sentiment Analysis using *Fallout: New Vegas* Dialog,' in *FDG '22: Proceedings of the 17th International Conference on the Foundations of Digital Games.*

Howard, Kenton Taylor. 2019. 'Romance Never Changes... or Does it?: Fallout, Queerness, and Mods,' in *DiGRA '19 – Proceedings of the 2019 International Conference.*

Howard, Kenton Taylor. 2021. 'Critical Modding: A Design Framework for Exploring Representation in Games,' PhD Dissertation, University of Central Florida.

Livingston, Christopher. 2018. '*Fallout 76* Review,' *PCGamer* (November 21), https://www.pcgamer.com/fallout-76-review/ (accessed January 30, 2023).

Morshirnia, Andrew V. and Walker, Anthony C. 2007. 'Reciprocal Innovation in Modding Communities as a Means of Increasing Cultural Diversity and Historical Accuracy in Video Games,' in *DiGRA '07 – Proceedings of the 2007 DiGRA International Conference: Situated Play.*

Pereira, Leônidas S. and Bernardes, Maurício M. S. 2022. 'Reporting on the Project Development Practices of Total Conversion Game Mod Teams,' in *Creative Industries Journal.*

Radian-Helix Media. 2020. 'Fallout – New California,' *Nexusmods* (April 8), https://www.nexusmods.com/newvegas/mods/45138/ (accessed January 30, 2023).

torcher. 2017. '*Fallout 4* Texture Optimization Project,' *Nexusmods* (February 8), https://www.nexusmods.com/fallout4/mods/978 (accessed January 30, 2023).

Tran, Edmond. 2018. '*Fallout 76* Review – No Humans Allowed,' *Gamespot* (November 25), https://www.gamespot.com/reviews/fallout-76-review-no-humans-allowed/1900-6417040/ (accessed January 30, 2023).

Wolf, Mark J.P. 2012. *Building Imaginary Worlds: The Theory and History of Subcreation.* London: Routledge.

Welch, Tom. 2018. 'The Affectively Necessary Labour of Queer Mods,' in *Game Studies* 18(3).

Yang, Robert. 2015. 'Radiator 1,' *Itch.IO,* https://radiatoryang.itch.io/radiator1 (accessed January 30, 2023).

Conclusion

Success and Failure, Design Strategies, and the Future of the World of Fallout

As I have demonstrated throughout this book, Fallout is a vast imaginary world: while it began with a single developer, Tim Cain, it has now become a popular video game franchise with entries from many video game developers. Much of the previous chapters of this book have therefore focused on specific Fallout video games with similarities in terms of design, theme, or other common elements. The first chapter looked at the original games by Interplay, the second looked at Bethesda's single-player games, and the third looked at spinoff games. The chapter before this one expanded that scope beyond video games and looked at Fallout fan creations more broadly, and while I touched on *Fallout 76* (2018), a video game that relies heavily on player-generated content, I also looked at video game mods and tabletop games, as the Fallout world has been expanded far beyond its original roots through player-generated content. Throughout the previous chapters I touched on nine video games, numerous mods, and all the various Fallout tabletop games, looking at many different ways in which the Fallout world has taken shape. Much like the introduction, this concluding chapter takes on a broader perspective: rather than focus on specific games, in the first section I instead analyze the successes and failures of world-building in the Fallout world overall. My goal in this section is not to praise or criticize particular games but instead to provide examples of things that worked well and things that did not for video game developers and for those who are building imaginary worlds more generally. In the second section of this chapter I look at design strategies and lessons for world-building that can be gleaned from the Fallout franchise. In particular, I look at Fallout's references to other forms of media: the franchise has been both criticized and praised for its various approaches to doing so. In addition, I look at *All Roads* (2010), a prequel comic depicting some of the events that transpired before

DOI: 10.4324/9781003395744-6

the beginning of *Fallout: New Vegas* (2010), and *Fallout Pinball*, an expansion pack for *Bethesda Pinball* (2016) that is only loosely connected to the Fallout world. I also briefly discuss the upcoming Fallout television show, though the show is untitled, its release date is still uncertain at the time of this writing, and details about it are relatively scarce at this point. Overall, in this chapter I argue that the Fallout world offers many useful examples to those building imaginary worlds and that valuable lessons can be learned from the Fallout franchise for creators working with imaginary worlds in almost any form of media.

25 Years of World-Building: Success and Failure in the Fallout Franchise

As mentioned in the introduction, at the time of this writing the Fallout world is a little over 25 years old: *Fallout 1* came out in 1997, and new entries in the franchise were relatively common other than a short period of dormancy in the mid-2000s. The series has seen many successes and failures over the years in terms of world-building: many elements of the Fallout series are iconic and serve as strong examples of how to successfully build an imaginary world, while others have clashed so much with the Fallout franchise's canon that they have been formally excluded from by the game's developers. As mentioned above, my goal in this section is not to criticize particular games or praise others, nor is it to attempt to categorically examine all kinds of success and failure in terms of Fallout's world-building: instead, I aim to provide some examples within the franchise as a whole. I argue that these successes and failures also inform the design strategies and lessons that I discuss in the next section of this chapter, such that an analysis of them provides a framework for looking at those ideas in the context of the Fallout's references to other forms of media and Fallout's actual forays into other forms of media.

In terms of world-building successes, one of the clearest successes of the franchise might be found in its aesthetic direction and consistency over a 25-year period. Fallout's 1950s retro futuristic aesthetic is quite iconic: more than anything else, that aesthetic is the element of the franchise that casual fans would immediately recognize. Lafleuriel (2018: 26) argues that "the thing that would elevate *Fallout* above the numerous other games and even the variety of sci-fi novels was its explosive mix of a post-apocalyptic setting and the retro style of 1950s America." Similarly, McClancy (2018) claims that "the games present a totalizing projection of the future as imagined by the past, and are famous for their retrofuturistic gameworld." It is particularly impressive that this aesthetic has been maintained throughout the entire Fallout series since the game series has gone through numerous iterations: Fallout games have been created by many different developers, have taken on wildly different gameplay styles, and have even seen entire overhauls in terms of world design between the early isometric games and the later open-world games. Throughout all of those iterations the franchise's tone, mood, and feel has been surprisingly consistent, which might suggest that these aesthetics are a core element of the franchise more than anything else: while gameplay might vary significantly when comparing two Fallout games from different points in the series' history, the franchise's unique art style and approach has seen very little change.

Another success might be seen in the Fallout franchise's "Perks" system, a mechanic which has inspired countless other systems in games. The system quite famously was invented extremely quickly, with Brian Fargo, head of Interplay during *Fallout 1*'s development, playing an early build of the game and requesting something to make leveling up more interesting (Cain, 2012). The developers came up with Perks, which are special benefits that can be gained while leveling up: for example, Silent Running offers the ability to remain stealthy while running, while Strong Back allows a character to carry more equipment. The system was created and implemented into *Fallout 1* in about a week (Cain, 2012) and has remained a key feature of Fallout games ever since, with almost every single Fallout game having some form of them. The term "perk" is now used for almost any similar system in other video games, even in completely different genres: first-person shooters like the Call of Duty franchise, survival games like *Deep Rock Galactic* (2020), and adventure games like *The Last of Us* (2013) all have similar in-game systems called with abilities called perks. It is difficult to trace the origins of the term to the Fallout franchise through scholarly sources, but sources like Wikipedia and Giant Bomb, a video game fan site, cite *Fallout 1* as the first instance of the term's usage, though most such sources also acknowledge that the perk system is clearly inspired by things like power-up systems in earlier video games. That being said, it is difficult to track down a use of the term "perk" to specifically refer to such a system before *Fallout 1*, and the widespread use of the concept in gaming in general could almost certainly be attributed to the popularity of the Fallout games and their pioneering usage of the idea.

In terms of failures of world-building, the Fallout franchise's primary issues can be found with the canonicity problems that I discussed in Chapter 3. In particular, it is again worth noting that the events of two spinoff games, *Fallout Tactics* (2001) and *Fallout: Brotherhood of Steel* (2004), are considered almost entirely noncanonical: the events of *Fallout Tactics* that remain canon were retconned to fit with canon established in later games, and the events of *Fallout: Brotherhood of Steel* have been explicitly declared noncanonical. While the games themselves are still interesting in terms of their contributions to the Fallout world, both games represent world-building failures in the sense that they are not necessarily even considered part of that world in an official sense. While the fan creations I discussed in the previous chapter are similarly not canonical and while there are some similarities between such expansions of Fallout world and Fallout spinoff games, the issues of the spinoff games being not canonical is more significant because of their more official aura: fan creations should not necessarily be held to the same standards as commercially released video games.

It is also worth noting that games like the Fallout franchise have another problem in terms of maintaining canonicity as well: the games offer players many different potential choices during their narrative. These choices create a wide range of outcomes for a particular game's story, such that future games must account for those outcomes in some way. This problem is not uncommon with choice-based games: Bethesda's own The Elder Scrolls series, for example, has the same issue. The question, of course, is how to account for this situation, and different game series have tried different approaches: The Elder Scrolls addresses the issue by using settings that are very far apart in terms of distance and time frame, allowing subsequent games to make references to previous ones by briefly mentioning some of the most notable events in their respective stories that will occur in every playthrough of the game. The Fallout games, on the other hand, all take place within the United States and occur over a period of less than 200 years, meaning that the events of their respective games occur in a relatively compressed setting in terms of time and space. In addition, the outcomes of stories in Fallout games can typically vary quite dramatically, making it more difficult to provide a canonical version of events that does not clash with some of the potential outcomes in the games. While the post-apocalyptic setting in Fallout places some limitations on communication, the events of previous games naturally come up at some point in subsequent games, and in general the Fallout series handles this by simply deciding upon a particular canonical outcome for some of the choice-based stories in any previous games. The best example of this might be the Shady Sands-Khans storyline that I discussed in Chapter 1: *Fallout 2*'s (1998) story is constructed based on the assumption that the main character of *Fallout 1* resolved that story by wiping out almost all of the Khans and saving the town of Shady Sands. Of course, it is possible to resolve that storyline in other ways and *Fallout 2* could have simply left the situation open-ended, but since significant elements in the Fallout world are impacted by that storyline *Fallout 2* took the approach of offering a canonical version of what happened in *Fallout 1*.

Finally, before discussing design strategies that can be learned from the world of Fallout, I want to note here that the examples discussed in this section are not necessarily intended to be instructive in terms of demonstrating specific lessons about world-building. Fallout's issues with canonicity, for example, provide a useful illustration of a world struggling to manage its own canon but do not necessarily suggest that a world that has many creators involved will automatically have such problems. Wolf (2012: 270) discusses the varying levels of canonicity of the Star Wars franchise, which I compared to the Fallout franchise in previous chapters, but I would not argue that Star Wars suffers from similar problems: in fact, I would suggest that the creators of Fallout might be able to look to Star Wars as an example of how to manage its own canon! Instead, the elements I discuss in this section are intended to provide examples of success and failure in terms of world-building, while in the next section I discuss some design strategies for world-building based on Fallout's references to and expansions into others forms of media.

How I Learned to Stop Worrying and Launch the Bombs: World-Building Design Strategies from the World of Fallout

As mentioned above, Fallout has had many successes and failures in world-building, and many design strategies can be drawn from how the Fallout world is designed. One design strategy that can be gleaned from looking at the Fallout world is how the franchises handle references to other media, something that the Fallout games do quite frequently. This has changed dramatically over time: *Fallout 1* mostly relies on relatively subtle nods to other forms of media, with its most overt perhaps being the appearance of Dogmeat, a dog character whose name directly references the nickname of a dog in *The Road Warrior* (1981). *Fallout 2* has more overt jokes that often break the fourth wall, such as the "Bridgekeeper" encounter, a direct reference to *Monty Python and The Holy Grail* (1975), during which the player comments "for some reason, I think I should save my game in a brand new slot" (Black Isle, 1998). *Fallout 3* (2008) deliberately moved away from such overt jokes, using the approach used in *Fallout 1* as an inspiration and again relying more on small nods to other franchise, an approach Bethesda used again in *Fallout 4* (2015) and *Fallout 76* (2018). It is also worth mentioning the particularly interesting approach used in *Fallout: New Vegas* (2010): the game features an option that can be chosen during character creation called "Wild Wasteland." Choosing this option alters some content in the game, replacing it with the kinds of overt references to other media found in *Fallout 2*. While such an approach is not necessarily available to all forms of imaginary worlds, it offers a unique design strategy to video game designers, who could potentially use a similar approach: doing so allows those who are bothered by such references to avoid them entirely, while those who do not mind references to other media can optionally toggle them on.

A design strategy can also be drawn from the Fallout franchise by looking at Fallout Pinball, an expansion pack for *Bethesda Pinball* (2016), a virtual pinball game that offers various game boards based on popular Bethesda franchises such as The Elder Scrolls. The expansion pack's connection to the Fallout world is relatively surface level, as the story of the game is effectively a retelling of the events of *Fallout 4* that blends some elements of Fallout's mechanics with those of a pinball game, such that it does not actually expand the world of Fallout in any new way. While the expansion pack's content is mostly drawn from *Fallout 4*, it does feature characters and content from across the Fallout games, making references to the larger Fallout world as well. Such an approach may seem to be relatively shallow, as Fallout Pinball could be seen as nothing more than a way to sell copies of *Bethesda Pinball* to Fallout fans and/or to get pinball fans interested in the Fallout franchise, but the strategy Bethesda used was successful in that it allowed the expansion pack to avoid many of the problems that plagued other Fallout spinoff games in terms of canonicity. Fallout Pinball has no such problems because it works within mechanical and aesthetic elements already established in the franchise and does not try to tell a new story, essentially playing it safe in terms of Fallout canon. Fallout Pinball therefore offers a different kind of lesson to those building imaginary worlds, as it demonstrates the value of knowing when a world should not be expanded within a new medium: it would likely be difficult to tell a completely new and fully compelling story that is in line with the themes of the Fallout world within the context of a pinball game, so Bethesda simply opted to avoid telling a new story entirely.

Another useful lesson can be seen in how the Fallout world has been handled in non-game media. At this time of this writing there is only one piece of in-universe Fallout media that has been released: *All Roads,* a prequel comic set roughly one week before the events of *Fallout: New Vegas* begin. The events of *All Roads* are considered canonical and are generally quite consistent with the events of the game itself: when weighed against the problems with canonicity in Fallout spinoff games that I touched on in Chapter 3, the fact that the comic does not contradict the events of the game is certainly impressive. The comic remaining consistent with the events of the game might be attributed to the fact that Chris Avellone, one of the game's senior designers, was also the lead writer for the comic. Taking such an approach as opposed to outsourcing the comic therefore allowed the game's developers to ensure that nothing in the comic contradicts the game. Avellone and the other comic writers also used a specific approach in the comic: they avoided depicting the player-character of *Fallout: New Vegas* entirely. Avellone (2010) noted that "we decided not use the Courier in the book. We want the players to determine how their character looks, acts, and reacts so in the book we focused on the player's adversaries and the folks who want you dead" (George, Schdeen and Iverson, 2010). The approach taken in *All Roads* illustrates some useful design strategies for world-builders who are creating spinoff content in another medium, especially those creating prequel content. One strategy is having a direct connection between the creators of the original work and the spinoff when possible: Avellone's contributions to the comic's story were likely one main reason for why that story was consistent with the story of *Fallout: New Vegas*. Another strategy is considering what should not be depicted in prequel content: while I would not suggest that a main character should never appear in a prequel, that strategy certainly worked well for *All Roads,* especially since players of *Fallout: New Vegas* can choose their character's gender and appearance at the start of the game: that approach ensured that the events of the comic were consistent with the game. An approach that ensures consistency with the Fallout games will also be important for the upcoming Fallout television show and any future games, which I discuss in the concluding section of this chapter.

Please Stand By: The Future of the World of Fallout

To close this chapter, considering some of these lessons in light of the upcoming Fallout TV show, which will be the second piece of non-game Fallout media, allows for a sketch of what a successful version of the show might look like. While a TV show's success could be measured based on the show's viewer numbers or profitability, from a world-building perspective one measure of the show's success might be how well it functions within the Fallout canon overall, especially since *All Roads,* the Fallout franchise's only other expansion into non-game media, is considered canonical. Not contradicting elements of established canon is therefore a necessity, which opens up some possibilities for how the show might approach that issue: the show could follow the plot of one of the games much like Fallout Pinball does, recreating it in a TV format and being careful to portray events that are faithful to the game's events. In this form, the show would essentially act as a televised version of one potential playthrough of one of the games, since each game's plot depends on the actions of the player and is not necessarily set in stone: the show would therefore not be contradicting canon as it would simply be portraying one potential outcome of the game's story. This does not appear to be the approach the show is taking, however: details about the show are still relatively scare, it is still in early development, and the information that is available does not come directly from the showrunners, but comments from Bethesda's Todd Howard on a recent podcast (Broadwell, 2022) suggest that the show will tell an entirely new story within the world of Fallout. I discuss the potential issues with that approach below.

Since the currently available information suggests that the Fallout TV show will be depicting an entirely new story, it is worth noting that the approach it will be taking might be more challenging than simply following the plot of one of the existing games: not only does it create the problem of needing to not contradict established Fallout canon, it also introduces a new issue in that this version of the show needs to be careful not to establish anything that might be a problem later within the canon as well. This issue crops up in many television shows already: famously, *Star Trek: The Next Generation* (1987–1994) introduced a "speed limit" on space travel in a Season 7 episode called "Force of Nature," which leads to the show having to create reasons for why ignoring the speed limit was necessary in future episodes – and eventually simply abandoning the idea altogether in future Star Trek television shows. Issues like this are why much of *Fallout: Brother-hood of Steel* is considered noncanonical: the game established world elements like the main character of *Fallout 1* appearing in Texas that either had to be accounted for or eliminated from the franchise canon, and in most cases subsequent games chose the latter option. Finally, the show needs to capture the feel of the Fallout franchise effectively. Doing this is important because the world of Fallout has a specific tone, and things that clash with that tone are often quite striking: for example, one major criticism of *Fallout: Brotherhood of Steel* was the use of a soundtrack featuring metal bands from the late 1990s and early 2000s rather than the popular music of the 1940s, 1950s, and 1960s that the franchise was typically known for. On the other hand, *Fallout: New Vegas* was able to incorporate contemporary music from the 1990s and 2000s alongside the usual older popular music typically used in the franchise because most of that music was country- and western-oriented, which matched closely with the game's setting in the western United States and the overall tone of the franchise. As such, it is certainly possible for the show to remain consistent with established Fallout canon and the aesthetics of its world, though its writers may want to look more closely at spinoff media like *All Roads* rather than spinoff games like *Fallout: Brotherhood of Steel*.

Overall, the Fallout TV show faces many challenges: many of those challenges are the same difficulties that any adaptation faces, and video game adaptations have already been notoriously difficult to pull off effectively. Overcoming the typical difficulties of adaptation while also managing the additional challenges of respecting the estab-lished Fallout canon and not establishing anything that might be prob-lematic for that canon is certainly a tall order, though the showrunners currently connected to the show have a good deal of experience. The worst outcome in this scenario is that the Fallout TV show follows in the footsteps of games like *Fallout: Brotherhood of Steel*, becoming seen as a mostly noncanonical expansion of the world. On the other hand, a well-done TV show would be an effective expansion of the show, perhaps getting referenced in future games such as *Fallout 5*, a game which is in very early stages of production, though essentially nothing is known about it other than the fact that it is being developed by Bethesda. Either way, the world of Fallout offers a lot of lessons to creators, as I have illustrated in this chapter: perhaps the best way forward for the television show creators, as well as anyone else involved in the franchise, is to ensure that they have learned those lessons as they continue in the tradition of expanding the world of Fallout as so many have done before. Similarly, world-builders of all kinds can draw on these design strategies as they build their own imaginary worlds: as *The World of Fallout* has shown, building imaginary worlds always changes.

References

Black Isle. 1999. *Fallout 2: A Post Nuclear Role Playing Game.* Interplay Productions.

Broadwell, Josh. 2022. 'The Fallout TV Show Tells a New Story in the Survival RPG's Universe,' *USA Today* (December 1), https://ftw.usatoday.com/2022/12/fallout-tv-show-story (accessed January 30, 2023).

Cain, Tim. 2012. 'Classic Game Postmortem: Fallout,' *GDCVault.* https://www.gdcvault.com/play/1015843/Classic-Game-Postmortem (accessed January 30, 2023)

'Experience Point,' *Wikipedia*, https://en.wikipedia.org/wiki/Experience_point (accessed January 30, 2023).

George, Rich, Schedeen, Jesse and Iverson, Dan. 2010. 'SDCC10: Fallout New Vegas Origins,' in *IGN Comics* (July 20), https://web.archive.org/web/20100809123743/ http://comics.ign.com/articles/110/1107292p1.html (accessed January 30, 2023).

Lafleuriel, Erwan. 2018. *Fallout: A Tale of Mutation: Creation – Universe – Decryption.* Toulouse: Third Editions.

McClancy, Kathleen. 2018. 'The Wasteland of the Real: Nostalgia and Simulacra in Fallout,' in *Game Studies*, 18(2).

'Perk,' *Giant Bomb*, https://www.giantbomb.com/perk/3015-366/ (accessed January 30, 2023).

Wolf, Mark J. P. 2012. *Building Imaginary Worlds: The Theory and History of Subcreation.* London: Routledge.

Index

For Product Safety Concerns and Information please contact our EU
representative GPSR@taylorandfrancis.com
Taylor & Francis Verlag GmbH, Kaufingerstraße 24, 80331 München, Germany